MW01254281

Marching Bands Make Me Cry

~

Hearing Drumbeats
and Choosing Your Tribe

BOB BRODSKY

The cover snapshot of Robert Putnam Brodsky (the author) and Sara Jane Williamson (Sally Hoffman), taken in Leonardo, NJ, ca.1942, is from a hand-colored 8" x 10" enlargement, referred to on page 4.

ISBN 0-9610914-3-6
Published by Brodsky & Treadway, P.O. Box 335, Rowley, MA 01969 U.S.A.
BobBrodsky@comcast.net   Telephone 1-978-948-7985

Design, compositing, and photographic services by
Higgins & Ross, Lowell, MA. photodesign@comcast.net
Printed by Thomson-Shore, Dexter, Michigan, USA

PREFACE

This memoir is about my journey to distinguish myself from the image my parents set before me. Not all closely-watched children find themselves on such a quest, but for the non-rebellious ones who do, there is one overriding awareness: other people help. Within this awareness, there is another factor that gradually raised some people in my consciousness.

My parents were generous and attentive to the end that their two sons should bring credit to them. My brother is six years older than I (but only five when I begged to accompany him to the movies). Dad, in his formalness, never disciplined me by force. Mom did. The fact that they were older when I was born (Mom 42, Dad 48) did not make it easier to define myself. I felt I owed a lot to my parents for their nurture. I am genuinely grateful for the many things they did for me, and I was prepared to help them in their old age, should they have needed me.

In accepting their judgments about me and my activities, I failed to develop a solid sense of who I was apart from them. I would not even be aware of this concept had it not been for the events I'm going to tell you about. Certain people were key to these events, and they were all outside my family. I refused to acknowledge their significance for many years because all the events had troubling aspects. When I began to realize the importance of these people to me, I decided to write about them. I will call them "the Others."

Also, I will introduce you to many other folks outside my parents' circle who gave me exceptional benefits, afforded me opportunities, and involved me in their wisdom, crafts, hopes, fears, beliefs, and prejudices. But the Others did something different.

The Others sensed who I was as a personality—my native talents, inclinations, temperament, limitations—and they risked their own well-being, their employment, and their other relationships to make me aware, by word and gesture, of what they observed. How could such simple acts put them at risk? I will tell you later, but first, let me say it again a little differently: the Others did what they did and said what they said because of who they perceived me to be, and they did it through an event of the moment—that for me gradually became a transforming event. They showed me to myself, and it rang true in one way or another, sometimes "yes!", sometimes "uh oh."

The Others almost never told me what to do, but they could have lost their jobs over what they did tell me. No small consideration. However long or brief my relationship with them, the important stuff occurred decisively.

Ironically, at those times and maybe for many years afterward, some of those events seemed like train wrecks. To see myself as I didn't know myself before—was unnerving. It took me about thirty years to gain my footing.

During those years I often thought about the Others. Until I was about fifty years old, I regarded them as marginal influences.

Then, I began to realize that the changes I was beginning to make in my life resulted from their influences upon me. Holy Cow! Maybe they were really Somebodies, at least for me.

Slowly, I identified five Others. I wrote this volume to name them, to tell of the little yet catalytic events we were involved in, and to honor them—to honor them because those events would not have happened had they not been who they were in that moment. Along my way I uncovered a deep well of gratitude toward my own family and many other people in my life, some who appear in this writing and many who don't.

Writing this out has been difficult, so I've employed the metaphor of different kinds of drumming (something I'm fondly acquainted with) to give you clues to understanding each chapter. They are, in order:

FLAMS—drum beats one can't ignore;

RUFFS—Mom and Dad's predictable rudiments;

PARADIDDLES—even beats, yet different;

SYNCOPATIONS—disruptions that affect your breathing;

HAND DRUMMING—drumming to embrace the terror.

Bob Brodsky
January 2005

Flams

—DRUM BEATS ONE CAN'T IGNORE

Flams make a lot of noise. While a marching band is on parade, both sticks come down on the drums slightly out of sync with each other, a grace note preceding a big strike. You know flams as the ominous tenor drum beats in state funerals, and on happier occasions with the snares tensioned, two pairs of flams followed by a roll and another pair of flams tell you the whole band is about to begin playing. There is one event in my past that has stood out like two flams.

When I was in my mid-thirties, some thirty-five years ago, I went through a career change that was really a lot more than that, resulting in the dissolution of my marriage and the disruption of my family's life. It was awful; I thought I was going nuts. I think now it was precipitated by my father's death.

While visiting my brother's family over Christmas a year later, I learned that Miss Edna A. Brandenburg, the astute principal of my elementary school, was still alive, living in a retirement home in California. I dropped her a note describing the changes in my life. She wrote back immediately, describing a conversation she had with my brother and his wife some years before:

I don't suppose Putnam or Peggy ever told you that
I was upset when I learned you were headed for the
ministry. Put said, seriously, 'Why not, if that's
what he wants?' 'I'm afraid he'll become frustrated,'
I replied, 'a brilliant, creative boy like Bob.'

    Did you?

I recall Miss Brandenburg as a wise and canny person, so to be
called "brilliant" by her confused me. I never thought of myself as very
intelligent. Maybe she was becoming a little dotty. But that she thought
of the Christian ministry as an inappropriate vocation for a person
with a creative bent, had never occurred to me. Suddenly, some things
began to make sense.

    I was in hot water with my congregations from the start. After
I gave a Lord's Supper meditation about being caught with evidence of
Jesus' execution in our hands, one of the congregation leaders told me
she nearly threw up. Then, there was the Easter morning I had the
ushers pass out the Order of Worship folders, only this time they were
blank inside except for the name of the church, the date, and the
week's announcements. On that bright morning I was trying to repli-
cate a little of the shock of the empty tomb of Jesus. The congregation
knew the order of worship very well, and they didn't need printed
directions every week. But I also knew they liked to be led over the
familiar path, and some even took pride in having a printed record of
the hymns sung, the scripture read, and the sermon title—or maybe
just that they'd been to church. So, this Easter I gave them a little test
of faith: could they worship God without the printed guide? Not a big
risk, just an exercise to build confidence in their ability to carry on

when life changes—certainly not as shocking as the empty tomb of Jesus was reported to have been.

Well, even those who got my point thought I'd gone completely over the edge. One woman called me crying, saying she wouldn't resign her church membership but she'd lost friends trying to defend my prank. She wasn't kidding. Some months later she hanged herself, and I feel in some way accountable for undermining her. Miss Brandenburg was right; I was not the guy for that kind of job.

I was not brought up to be a minister but rather a soldier—to dwell among the officer class. There were two generals on Mom's side of the family: one from The War Between the States (Robert Nugent), and another from The War for Independence (Rufus Putnam). I was named after both of them, and she liked to remind me and tell others of this frequently.

Mom enrolled me in the children's division of the Daughters of the American Revolution. The local chapter met weekly after school for games and stories of our glorious past, followed by punch and cookies. I was selected for a role at the state convention. I was to play George Washington (Mary Louise Brown was Martha), and we were to take turns presenting corsages to the solemn ladies immediately after they had stepped to the podium, before they addressed the assembly. I was costumed in a high-collared ruffled shirt, knee britches, blue tailcoat, white wig topped by a tri-cornered hat, white stockings, and shoes appropriate to the Colonial period.

On returning from presenting a gardenia to one of the speakers, my foot snagged the electrical cord leading to the podium, plunging the speaker's text into darkness. When I bent over to reconnect the cord to its floor outlet, my tails parted, the rear seam of my tight satin britches split open wide, exposing white underwear, and the great hall erupted in uncharacteristic rolling laughter. I fled.

I turned red in embarrassment every time I recalled this event, even twenty years later. My lengthy embarrassment should have been a clue that I was stuck in my mother's expectations and didn't know how to get free. Had I become unstuck, I could have smiled at the memory. I could have shrugged it off as a learning experience, painful at the moment, and inevitable considering the circumstances. But I wasn't ready to see it that way; I was still ashamed of my performance. I thought the split in my pants should not have happened. At my young age I had already taken to heart such family phrases as, "I had no business...," and "I should have watched my step" (so as not to have kicked out the plug). Or, I should have left the darkness problem to a hotel employee. Something like that. Sally Hoffman, the niece of a woman who cared for me when I was little, knew about my quandary before I did:

> You know it's funny, over the years I have taken this picture out [*see the cover photo*], and I don't know why, I truly don't know why. I've taken it out, and I've looked at it, and I've often wondered what happened to the little boy that's in the picture. I look at the two faces of the children, the little girl (that's me) looks like she's just having a good time. She's really just enjoying the moment of being where she's being.
>
> But if you look closely at the face of the little

boy, if you look at his eyes, he looks like he's strain-
ing to get it right—'Am I O.K.? Am I O.K.?'—
more than having a good time and being relaxed.
And maybe that's why I've wondered about the picture and about the little boy in the picture. I've
wondered, 'What became of Robert Brodsky?' even
up until a few years ago.

I had heard that you had gone to Princeton. I had
heard that you had become a Presbyterian clergy.
I looked you up in the Presbyterian directory
when I was in my early fifties. It was this picture.
I kept wondering, 'What happened to that kid?'

So, why did I go into the ministry? The customary answer,
"I was called," wasn't true for me. I didn't hear any voices, see any
bushes burning inexplicably. During the spring of my senior year in
high school I had been confronted with a contentious event between
two people I respected, and my response was to put myself on a career
path to the ministry, a place in society from which I thought I could
help people sort things out before they leapt at one another's throats.
In front of the church elders I was urged to say I "believed" I was
"called." I was asked to speak in a form of code, acknowledging the
fundamentals of conservative Protestantism. I really didn't have the
required beliefs, even though I had been processed through the Sunday
School. So, I learned the code, fudged my way around the questions,
and found doors opening for me. I fed the church committees words they
wanted to hear. "Was Jesus my Lord and Savior?" "Yes, indeed." And
did I believe "the holy scriptures of the Old and New Testaments are

the word of God, the only rule of faith and obedience"? "Yes, indeed!"

My parents were intent on guiding my brother and me toward careers they could boast about. The ministry was not among them, but after a while they accepted my decision. My brother, while being urged to campaign for admission to West Point, had decided to become a physician. "Physician" was also O.K. with Mom and Dad. When it came time for me to announce my vocation for my high school yearbook, I wrote "law." I didn't know what else to say. Dad was proud of his law degree, so I knew that would calm my parents' anxieties, even though I was not attracted to the legal profession.

Until I was five I ate supper at a low table in my bedroom. Mom made a point of putting real silverware on a little tablecloth. Usually she would sit with me while I tried to eat correctly. She was fond of telling friends that she took up smoking because I was such a slow eater. Mom, Dad, and my brother ate later. When I had graduated to having dinner in the dining room, I was taught to hold my mother's chair and attempt to push her up to the table. She was heavy. When we ate out, I sometimes held my mother's chair, and I learned to stand up whenever friends of my parents stopped by our table. The friends were impressed. My classmate Marilyn Hughes Johnson, recalling high school years, said:

> Indeed, he was the mothers' favorite, because when
> we were growing up, Bob would come into the
> house and shake hands with the parents and speak
> to them. A lot of other guys would kind of hang

back or not come into the house at all and not greet the parents. So, Bob was the kind of guy every mother wanted her daughter to go out with.

It never occurred to me that winning approval from my girl-friends' parents could stand between me and their daughters. I was so busy practicing what I had been taught, I never found out what the girls were about. I just assumed my behavior was what mattered. I was concerned with making a good impression that would find its way to my parents, and that girls, too, would like me for this. The chemistry of romance escaped me.

My deference toward elders exposed me to some rough teasing and made me an easy mark for bullies. Once, at Sunday dinner, my grandfather so humiliated me I slid from my chair in tears and sat alone under the table for a long time. I have no memory of what he said.

During fifth grade I fell in love with a classmate who lived on Tulip Street, one of the two half-mile routes to Brayton School. Elenita Jones was sophisticated beyond my imagination: she had lived in Switzerland. Unfortunately, she now lived next door to other class-mates, the McCarthy brothers, George and Larry, who took exception to my interest in their neighbor. George was fifteen pounds heavier and stronger than anyone else in my class, and joined by another class-mate, Bob Tomb [say "Tom"], the troubled son of the YMCA director, they would lie in wait for me and my friends from "up the hill" to kick and punch the livin' daylights out of us on our way home from school.

After several assaults, I decided to try to put an end to the attacks by proposing a "peace treaty," written by me, and to be signed by all parties in front of a real heavy, Miss Brandenburg. The treaty stated that the "up the hill" boys would be friends with the other boys if they would stop waylaying us. (Elenita was fading from the picture by then.) I went to Miss Brandenburg, and she agreed to let me give it a try. We were all summoned to Miss Brandenburg's office. She turned the meeting over to me. The McCarthy boys and Bob had nothing to say when given the opportunity. We all signed. Miss Brandenburg witnessed and kept the document. The "peace treaty" worked, though it was hard to be friends with George and Larry.

When I entered puberty, a lump appeared under one of my nipples. Mom had left a women's magazine in the bathroom that bannered an article on breast cancer. I read it and then prayed mightily that if God would just make the lump go away, I would try harder to be a good kid. The lump didn't go away, so eventually I mentioned it to my dad, and he took me to see Dr. Maroney.

I knew the solemn Dr. Maroney from frequent bouts with the common cold, but this day he was in rare humor. He examined the trouble spot, then pronounced that I had nothing to worry about—it was just that I was going to be a girl.

I don't recall either my father or Dr. Maroney saying anything to calm the panic the doctor had visited upon me, but I'm sure I let out an exclamation, a "Huh?" or "What?" and they assured me I had nothing to worry about. Little did they know!

Gender confusion, though it probably lasted but a moment, sent me into a tailspin. I was not inclined to put on a dress until, in high school with two other guys, we consented to impersonate The

Andrews Sisters and lip-sync "Hold Tight" for a YWCA variety show, and by that time I was no longer Dr. Maroney's patient.

At the dinner table Dad would frequently ask, rather playfully, "Tell us what you've been up to today. Give an account of yourself." Sometimes my accounts included spirited exaggerations, and Dad would respond, "Sounds like a thousand cats on the backyard fence," referring to the tall tale of a feline jamboree he reported to his father in the eighteen-nineties—and was mildly censured for.

Unlike Dad, Mom had no tolerance for my fibbing. My first recollection of the full power of her wrath occurred when I began kindergarten.

In my excitement at entering school, I took a short-cut across a new home site. Running atop a pile of yellow clay, I slipped on the goo. Muddy from the waist down, I ran back home to clean up and start over. Mom caught up with me in the bathroom and demanded to know *how* I could have so soiled my pants. When I told her where I'd been, she said I had no business going there. There didn't seem to be any room in Mom's face for me to say I was sorry I'd slipped, so I said I thought I was pushed. Mom instantly wanted to know who pushed me. Trapped and panicky, I said I didn't see who pushed me, and at my tangle of lies Mom began slapping my face all over. She finished by forcing the bar of soap into my mouth.

The day Mom so wounded me had begun in considerable excitement. When I showed up at the breakfast table that morning, I announced with pride that I'd made my bed. Mom responded,

"That's wonderful! Now you can make your bed *every* day." I felt she skipped over something there, too.

In fourth grade I learned there was going to be a school band, so I asked for and received drumming lessons from the teacher, Roy Fulmer. Mr. Fulmer was an all-around musician, recently discharged from a military band. Finally, I was doing something Mom and Dad approved of, and they bought me a snare drum. A good street beat played well is exhilarating. I remember how, in the high school marching band, we used to work on single stroke rolls—not the open or crushed double bounce of each stick but a controlled roar made with individual strokes. We would stand around the back of the band room or beside the band bus and try to do them easy and smooth. You had to feel the strokes as triplets, otherwise they lost their effect.

Although I was not one of the more coordinated drummers, at home I had learned my family's rudiments quite well (though my sense of timing there also left something to be desired).

Sally Hoffman (née Williamson) and I shared her aunt, Sara Sykora, to our enduring benefit in our early years. Having a secure adult with whom to enjoy the excitement of youthful discoveries and to whet our appetites for learning, gave us the best possible start.

When in school together, it never occurred to me that Marilyn Johnson (née Hughes) and I were not of the same social class. My good manners impressed her parents. On warm days Marilyn and I enjoyed popping tar bubbles in the gutter beside my house and twisting the black gooey stuff onto sticks.

I don't suppose Putnam or Peggy ever told you that I was upset when I learned you were headed for the ministry. Put said seriously Why not, if that's what he wants? I'm afraid he'll become frustrated, a brilliant, creative boy like Bob. Did you?

Brayton Elementary School Principal Edna Brandenburg avoided publicity. (The school superintendent didn't approve of women as principals). Hence, no photos. When we corresponded in 1980, her acute memory remained intact although her failing eyesight and penmanship revealed her advanced age.

On hearing one of my sermons, a colleague likened the experience to a duck hunter watching a flock rise before him—too much of a good thing. In the pulpit I wore an open robe to signify a caregiver's relationship to the congregation. I never wore the academic hood in public; it would have signaled status above role.

THE SIXTY-NINTH REGIMENT AT FREDERICKSBURG.

GENERAL NUGENT'S DESCRIPTION OF THE SPLENDID WORK THAT
WAS PERFORMED BY THE IRISH BRIGADE BEFORE
MARYE'S HEIGHTS, DECEMBER 11–15, 1862.

In spite of the exceedingly creditable record made by the Sixty-ninth Regiment at the battle of Fredericksburg, Va., in December, 1862, the only mention found in the Official Records of the Rebellion is contained in the subjoined paragragh—the only official report made for the regiment, by Captain James Saunders:

"In compliance with general orders received December 2, I hereby certify that the Sixty-ninth Regiment, New York Volunteers, entered the battle of Fredericksburg, on December 13, 1862, commanded by Colonel Robert Nugent, and 18 commissioned officers and 210 rank and file, in which the above numbered regiment lost 16 commissioned officers and 160 rank and file, leaving Captain James Saunders, Lieutenant (Robert H.) Milliken and Lieutenant L. (Luke) Brennan to bring the remnant of the regiment off the battle-field."

The fact has been established that the bodies of men from this organization, with sprigs of boxwood in their hats, were found nearest the stone wall at Marye's Heights. The following entertaining and instructive narrative from the pen of General Robert Nugent, U.S.A., was written at the request of this office, to fill a historical gap.

GENERAL NUGENT'S NARRATIVE.

Some thirty-six years ago the first regiment of an Irish Brigade took departure from the great metropolis, to the National Capital, to engage in a conflict on the very threshold of a great internecine war that was to determine the destinies of this great Republic.

A bloody mess. None of the Union troops escaped without wounds. Nugent was shot in his side.

As a young girl, Mom spent time with Grandpa Nugent, but she had few stories to tell, except of his Manhattan home burning during the 1863 draft riots, when he was a draft marshall there. He had his detractors within the military, also. I discovered he spent his last years defending himself in the New York newspapers for taking command of the Irish Brigade at the assault on Marye's Heights.

At the Children of the American Revolution Convention in Trenton, New Jersey, April 4, 1943, I became painfully acquainted with the Republican penchant for pageantry. I was costumed as a lordly Washington, and with Mary Louise Brown as Martha, commissioned to present corsages to the passionate women speakers. In the depths of the Second World War we were all God and Country, but the righteous members of that patriotic society would have found me a problem as I grew older had I not already embarrassed myself by splitting my pants.

My parents' romance was enlivened by Dad's complex observations and his elegant turns of phrase. He attempted to train me in elocution. Leading a junior high school assembly, I once amused the students by announcing Colonel Woodward, our principal, had some "miscellaneous comments" to make.

Sunday School prompted great attention to dress and grooming. My brother and I learned respect for ceremony, but the religious messages raised unanswerable questions, and my mind drifted away.

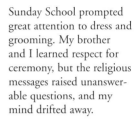

At this table Mom tried to teach me to eat correctly. My favorite foods were baked potatoes and overcooked chocolate pudding, both of which lent themselves to subsurface excavations. She told her friends my dallying over food drove her to chain smoke.

15

Ruffs

Now I lay me down to sleep,
I pray the Lord my soul to keep.
When in the morning light I wake,
Help me the path I love to take,
And keep the same for Thy dear sake.
God bless Mommy, and Daddy, and Nanny,
and Pop-Pop,
And all my friends and relatives make me a
good, strong boy.

Those last two lines rhythmically set a circle of family advisers over my bed. I must not disappoint them. Mom and Dad taught me to say the Lord's Prayer (Protestant version) and the "Now I lay me...." (their version) at a very early age. They required a morning and a goodnight kiss (on the lips). They practiced being in agreement in their responses to anything my brother or I asked of them. Comparing their parental behavior to drumming rudiments, I found them like a ruff: a totally consistent left-right-LEFT or right-left-RIGHT three stroke rudiment. It's the basis of the street beat the drum section plays at the very end of a parade, after the band has finished playing, while the weary musicians amble back to the bus or the band room, the snare drummers on autopilot, the bass drummer hardly able to lift one arm, the cymbal player weighed down with his Zildjians. Dad once said to me when my own children were being rambunctious, "Children are like wild animals, they have to be civilized." The implication was quite clear: I needed to discipline my children. Br-r-rump.

One bit of perspective I was afforded came from having an older brother. Put was someone I could go to the movies with, generally bug when I was at loose ends, and the one who took most of the heat from any misfortune that befell common endeavors.

I was present at family trials of my brother for minor and major misbehavior, but when he was sent off to military school, I became the principal target for redress. Mom, weary from attempting to bring me up to her expectations, would seek out advice from our next door neighbor, Faith Stranad. Faith told me:

> She worried more about Put out loud, and that's
> what gave me the clue that she wasn't always mad at
> you. I honestly believe that in my bones. She'd
> think he was going to fail or go with certain girls
> who were not going to make him successful if he
> got involved. And he wasn't the age to be, and that
> was another worry.
>
> And I always got the feeling—and I still have
> it—that when she was angry at you, you did not
> talk back. I don't know if you showed it, how you
> felt, but you said she could get very angry. And I

thought, 'She doesn't know that it isn't Bob that's making her so mad. She's in anguish over something Put is doing, which would remind her of him.' I don't know if she knew he was going to be a doctor then.

I always felt, 'Oh, poor Bob. If he only knew.' And I cannot tell people, because what if I'm wrong? I just can't do it.

Our parents' ambition for us led to some memorable occasions. I have a vivid recollection of finding Dad sitting on the grassy curb in front of our house one Saturday afternoon, talking with handyman Lafayette Grisby while Mr. Grisby waited for a ride back to the poor families' neighborhood in the center of town. We didn't call it a ghetto, but that's what it was. Dad was helping me pursue my interest in photography by hiring Mr. Grisby to install plumbing in my darkroom. When I joined the two men on the curb, I heard Dad telling of his concern that my brother be admitted to Princeton. I recall both Mom and Dad spilling their hearts out to hired help, but this particular conversation stuck in my mind. Mr. Grisby, who had a large family to feed, took Dad's angst in stride. He told my father that he must not be anxious for my brother's future, that if he didn't get into Princeton, he could surely go to another college that might be just as suited to his particular personality and talents. The only hint of Lafayette's unease was in his pulling up grass while he talked to Dad.

One of Mr. Grisby's children went on from high school to Colgate University, to the Harvard Graduate School, to the United States Information Agency as a Specialist in Eastern European Affairs, and finally, to the U.S. Department of Labor—achievements that could make any father proud. That child, also named Lafayette, gave me a different picture of life in our hometown and some of the important societal changes taking place, a picture I wouldn't have recognized if I didn't know to whom I was listening:

> Up through my fifth grade in elementary school, I had attended an all-black school. Even though I don't remember all of the circumstances as to why it was a black school, my speculation is that the school district lines were sort of gerrymandered to render such a school. For one thing, there was a school that was closer to where I lived, but that was an all-white school. The school that I attended was Hamilton School. The nearby school that those in my neighborhood thought that we should be attending was Lincoln School. At various times we would go past the school and a conflict would arise.
>
> As happens in life many times, irony steps in and has a joke on us, and that happened in this instance. At the end of my fifth-grade year, our school was permanently closed, the students were distributed to other existing elementary schools and the people in my immediate neighborhood were assigned to Lincoln School. We couldn't believe it. The summer before going, we kept reminding ourselves of what an ordeal was going to be in store for us when the summer was over. What one has to remember is that this was taking place during World War II, and as boys

were wont to do, we often played soldiers and commandos and we many times played that we were training for war. At various times over that summer when we were doing such playing, we would say, 'Remember, we've got to strengthen up and build up our muscles, and be ready for going to Lincoln School because we know that they are really going to take it out on us and try to get back at us' (for the conflicts that had occurred over the years).

Finally, the first day of school came, and all of us, that is all of the black students who were assigned to Lincoln School, went together. I've forgotten the number, but it was probably approximately twenty boys and girls. We all went to school together. At that time, there was a boys playground and a girls playground. We left the girls at the girls playground, and told them not to bother anybody themselves, to go in and be quiet, but if anybody bothered them, to give a yell and we would be over to help them and to rescue them. The boys then proceeded over to the boys playground, and just as we had anticipated, the playground was full of boys. It looked as though virtually every boy in the school was there waiting for us. We said, 'Well this is it. It's no less, no more than what we expected.'

We proceeded to enter the playground, ready for anything, and as we approached, one of the fellows stepped out from the crowd. We stopped, and I, as sort of the unofficial leader of our group, stepped out to meet him. And we eyed each other for what seemed like a longer time than I'm sure it actually was, and he finally stuck out his hand and said, 'Hello, I want to welcome you to our school.' He said, 'I know that our two schools have had difficulties in the past, but now we're one school. You're part of our school now, and we want to welcome you.' We were all taken aback, but I must say, very pleasantly surprised. That really set the tone for what transpired for the remainder of the school year. There were a few incidents here and there, but overall, it was a very pleasant experience.

As it turned out, it was probably the most important year in my life because I had a very good experience in that school. I got introduced to people, some of whom I've maintained contact with to this day. Also, it let me see that I could perform academically as well as the students who were at that school. When we went to junior high school, I proceeded to take the same courses as they did, and ultimately, that led me to the college preparatory curriculum, and from there, on to college, and on to where I am at this present time.

But while young Lafayette and his siblings were becoming legends in the Summit, New Jersey, schools, Mom managed to keep our attention focussed on family matters. One night when I was about eight, I awakened to hear Mom yelling, "Not in all my life have I ever been treated this way!" She was shrieking at my father, and Dad was trying to calm her by saying her name over and over, "Dorothy. Oh, Dorothy."

Whatever offense had been committed, Dad didn't think it merited such a fuss. Mom headed down the hallway toward my brother's room at the far end of the house, shouting, "Putnam, Putnam, I want you to know *my* father would *never* allow me to be treated this way." From my sleepy state I couldn't figure out what my father had done that led to Mom's hysteria. I pulled the pillow tightly over my head and prayed with all my might that they would never get a divorce. I'd learned about the perils of divorce to children from my parents, and my insecurity in that moment was terrifying. My brother had a better grasp of the event:

> Dad didn't come home when he said he was going to come home; he'd been to a party. And Mother made a big deal out of this, saying, 'Goodness knows, you must have been running around with wild women.' I didn't know what she was talking about. I certainly didn't know about wild women, but after I thought about it, I thought that this was kind of fun, interesting to pursue. But anyhow, it was upsetting. It was very traumatic that night. She was running around the house, screaming and tearing her hair. And she made a big fuss. The whole thing blew over within a relatively short period of time. I have a sense that they didn't talk to each other for a few days, but after that life returned to normal.

It sort of bears out what I learned over many years of medical practice: that adults in positions of authority as far as children are concerned—parents screaming at each other, yelling at each other, fighting, is a terribly traumatic experience for a young child regardless of what the issue is (children don't know what the issue is). Very often they have no idea of the issue. It's just the fact of the commotion, the yelling between two people in authority who are of importance to the child. I don't think many adults realize how traumatic this can be unless they've been through it themselves. It's sad, but I've seen this many times and kids are truly scarred by this kind of thing.

I, too, recall that the next morning calm had been restored, and I dared not ask about the ruckus.

Both of my parents came from music-loving families, Dad from Czech-Austrian bureaucrats of the Upper East Side of New York, Mom from the manufacturing class of lower Manhattan. By the time they met, both families had migrated to Brooklyn. Their tastes ran toward classical music. Dad liked Wagner; Mom, César Franck and Tchiakovsky. Mom's post-high school education consisted of voice lessons. Young women of her class were kept on a very short leash. She might have done well in a business college, but college was not considered. Her trained voice proved good enough to hire out, but this was not allowed. She was encouraged to solo with church choirs and for her father's club buddies in Brooklyn and on the Jersey shore. To help her prepare, Pop-Pop gave her a piano. But as Dad had sold his cherished horse when he married Mom, Mom gave up singing when she left her parents' house. She still went to the piano occasionally to play the showy "Rustle of Spring," or a bit of Rachmaninoff, but that was it with the piano until my brother was old enough for lessons. Put recalls:

> The piano in the living room was at the foot of stairs, a back stairway to a balcony. And Mom would sit up there and read or knit or do something while I was practicing. It was her way of monitoring what I was doing, and if I hit a wrong note, she would holler out, 'Do that again' or 'That's not right.' So I'd do it again. And often it still wasn't right. Those were less happy periods in our relationship. And once they came to an end, I moved on to the clarinet, and moved out of the household, and things were better.

I, on the other hand, could entertain myself whenever I climbed onto the piano bench and pressed down the keys. Mom sent me off to study with a different teacher. Lessons consisted of exercises and attempts to play difficult pieces. When I made mistakes, Mom would complain, but I wasn't driven away from the keyboard as my brother had been. I would just stop for a while, rest my large front teeth on the edge of the piano case, then begin again.

I found the most comfort in the cellar with the electric trains where life's dramas seemed more manageable and where I might stay out of Mom's way. How wonderful the model village appeared when I turned off the basement lights, leaving only the little bulbs inside the moving cars, on the station platform, and in the houses and stores of the village. Every month a model railroad magazine arrived, and I learned to read trying to figure out what it said under the photos.

When my brother was sent away to military school to prepare him for officer rank in our war-wracked world, I took over his train set and immediately set about to make something more realistic with it. Dad approved of my ideas and brought me plaster, paint, and model shrubbery. But on two occasions the following year, I lifted money from Mom's pocketbook to finance other improvements: a freight house and a passenger station. Model kits cost far more than my weekly allowance. I was not paid for work around our house. It never occurred to me to do chores for neighbors for pay, so I stole the money from Mom's purse. Mom noticed my second theft and showed up at the door of my fifth grade classroom, beckoning me into the hallway. When I confessed, she slapped my face again and again, and called me everything I already knew I was. Then she opened the classroom door and shoved me, red-faced, back with my classmates.

When I went home that day, I was sent to my room with Mom's threats of reform school ringing in my ears. Seriously overwrought, she went next door to seek consolation from her friend, Faith. Mom returned, calling to me through the door, "Once a thief, always a thief."

Mom had called Dad at his office in New York, and when he arrived home that evening, I could hear her through the floor projecting my fate. Presently, Dad, in his three-piece suit with his Phi Beta

Kappa key dangling from his watch chain, came up to my room and sat down in the rocking chair. He didn't say anything at first. In what seemed a judgment of silence, he just looked at me. Then, staring out the window, he said how disappointed he was with me. Finally, he went downstairs and returned with my supper on a tray. I took it as an extraordinary act of kindness to a common criminal.

In the fifth grade I was appointed a street crossing guard but relieved of duty almost immediately because I was seen throwing a snowball at a car on my way home from school. Mom was reclining on her chaise lounge darning socks when I reported my dishonorable discharge. She looked up from her darning egg to say, "Robert, you're enough to drive a saint to distraction!"

Coming from a family of Prague Bohemians, Dad had a lively sense of theatrics, but he had a severe Austrian grandmother. The mix produced formal bureaucrats with a twist of hijinx. Dad's parents joined the conservative Missouri Synod Lutheran Church. His father earned enough as a German-speaking family lawyer to send his only child to New York University.

Once a year Dad and Mom dressed formally and went to The Metropolitan, meaning the Opera. And about once a month at the dinner table Dad would recall a moment of Wagner. As a lawyer working for an insurance company in lower Manhattan, Dad also used dinnertime to imbue us with maxims, such as "minimize your liabilities," and especially, "possession is nine-tenths of the law."

I was never at a loss to provoke commentary at the dinner table.

As a junior high student, I remember singing my way to the table one night with a song from the high school production of "Finian's Rainbow," which I'd watched in rehearsal. When I finished "That Great Come-and-Get-It-Day," Dad warned me not to take to heart any of Finian's "Tobacco Road" socialism. I didn't, but I didn't stop singing, either.

From the opposite end of the table, Mom seldom missed a chance to inveigh against Eleanor Roosevelt because Mrs. Roosevelt took the side of the arrogant idle poor. To justify her prejudice, Mom complained of being deliberately bumped in a department store elevator by a black woman whom she was sure had been led by Mrs. Roosevelt to do it. It seemed to me small recompense for the slights Mom dished out regularly to all blacks, poor whites, Irish Catholics, and Jews whom she didn't know personally.

For years Mom remained upset that the world-renowned singer Marian Anderson had applied to sing in the D.A.R. Constitution Hall. Mom said "she had no business" trying to book a concert there, and Mrs. Roosevelt had set race relations back for all time by getting in the middle of the fracas.

On the day President Roosevelt died, I remember Mom running down the stairs fretting mysteriously, "Oh, Truman, oh... that Truman!" President Truman suddenly became known around our house as "that little haberdasher from the Pendergast machine." When I learned what "haberdasher" meant, I realized how little respect Mom and Dad had for local merchants whom I really liked.

Mom and Dad did not hesitate to reveal their Republican opinions to the help or whenever they felt they were among allies. President Truman's advocacy of fair employment legislation brought

Mom's formidable anger to the surface. Senator Robert Taft was her man now, as Henry Ford had been in the '30s. Our dinner table was a place to learn the talk of preserving our advantages.

I was introduced to Dad's conservatism in the ceremony of hanging out the American flag on holidays. It meant law and order against anarchy. He preferred a moth-eaten forty-two star version from his infancy. In 1918, when women received the vote in New York, Dad had written to his mom from the battlefields of Belgium about how she should cast her first votes:

> You, Mother, must feel rather proud of your new
> right of franchise, and I hope you will have countless
> opportunities to exercise it—not all on one day
> though, remember. Whatever you do, when consid-
> ering how to vote on a proposition, do not get sym-
> pathetic. We need correct politics and economics,
> but above all the nearest possible approach to justice.

Dad, like some of our founding fathers, believed only educated white people of means should be allowed a voice in government. I found this out at age fourteen as we were sweeping the garage together. While I chattered of things I'd learned in social studies class about President Lincoln, he told me Negroes shouldn't be allowed to vote because if they did, "they'd outnumber us." It was a matter of their lack of education, he said, but I got an impression it was a lot more than that. Dad had written to his folks in Brooklyn of his WWI experience escorting a quartermaster company of black soldiers to France:

> We had two breezy days when the waves impressed
> on us that we were on a mighty ocean. The blacks

quickly got sick, and one announced with finality,
'I's gwine to be a European Nigger. I ain't comin'
back cross this yer water.' And so they go, these
simple brawny boys drafted from the cotton fields
of Virginia and the Carolinas. They are such children and obedient that we all rather like them.
I imagine they are as lazy as they come, though.

Public school exposed me to a variety of families' conditions
and their customs. When I talked about the kids of UN staffers who
showed up with Hindu caste markings, Mom and Dad informed me
that their parents were part of an organization that threatened
American sovereignty and that they belonged to a religion that did not
acknowledge the authority of Jesus. I can remember how nervous I
became talking with classmates or adults whom I was being taught to
distrust. I learned which friends I could bring home and which kids
I shouldn't even speak of at home.

During my brother's pursuit of college admission, he was told
by a colonel at his military school that "with a name like 'Brodsky' he
shouldn't expect to get into Princeton." This was all Mom needed to
hear to set her off on a two-front campaign to change our family name
to "Broderick" or "Bronson" and move us to the openly restricted
community of Smoke Rise, where Jews were not permitted. She began
saying she was tired of having to protest to department store clerks
when she gave them her charge card that she wasn't the wife of the
famous Hebrew jurist. Eventually, Mom's Smoke Rise idea drifted off,
and the name change campaign was also dropped when my brother
was finally admitted to Princeton just weeks before the fall semester.

To my puzzlement, throughout these years, my brother brought home high status Latino and Jewish classmates from both military school and Princeton, of whom Mom couldn't say enough good things.

Dad's parents died before I was born, but the influences of my mother's father more than made up for them. Grandfather Putnam had learned the high-class gestures. We saw each other every two weeks during the winter, and we lived next door during the summers at the New Jersey shore. Sundays in the winter began after church when Nanny and Pop-Pop would arrive in his limousine. I would follow Dad into the pantry where he made Old Fashioned cocktails for the adults and poured sherry for my brother and me. I got to muddle the bitters on the sugar cube in the Old Fashioneds and later eat the orange slices and maraschino cherries after the adults finished their drinks. When I was twelve, I took Pop-Pop's portrait on one of his Sunday visits. Nanny was a demure old lady, except for her stomach powders, which I watched her unfold and tap onto her tongue.

Pop-Pop would regale us with stories of the elegant styles of movie stars, such as Ronald Coleman, Paul Henried, and especially, Claude Raines. My grandfather owned a small rolling ladder factory on Troutman Street in Brooklyn and an iron facade office and warehouse on Howard Street, off Canal, in lower Manhattan. The New York Scotch-Irish and Dutchmen he traveled among were earnest clubmen, but more than club life, Pop-Pop enjoyed the romance of life aboard banana boats on which he escaped as often as business permitted. Usually leaving his wife in Brooklyn, he would take his marriageable daughter to the embassy ports of Latin America, where instead of finding a suitable husband, she would get dysentery.

To mark his 50th wedding anniversary, Pop-Pop threw a dinner party at the Waldorf-Astoria Hotel in New York. He invited his family, his old friends, and his business associates. I was seven at the time, and as I stepped out of an elevator, wearing a collarless jacket and short pants, a hotel guest exclaimed, "Oh, look at the little English boy!" I took it as a putdown, for how could someone descended from a general of the American Revolution be mistaken for an English boy? No one had bothered to explain that the Eaton get-up Mom bought for me was the uniform of young peers. In the confines of the banquet room I sought refuge among strolling musicians who were playing "Anchors Aweigh" for my Uncle Gair, on leave from the Navy. When it was time to find our places at the T-shaped table, a man appeared on a tall ladder with an enormous camera and directed us to adjust our chairs so each one could see him. Eventually, he set off a fearsome flash. Later Pop-Pop said some chummy things with his arm across the shoulders of Oscar Tschirky, the maitre d'hotel; and after roast beef, Pop-Pop read some touching things about his marriage, ending with " 'till death do us part." He then presented Nanny a ring of many little diamonds, and everyone applauded. I don't remember Nanny saying anything, then or ever. Throughout my parents' remaining years, that dinner party was the standard against which all other social events were measured—and they usually came up short.

Mom and Dad couldn't afford to throw big parties, but in the fall of each year Mom led us to one of the large family hotels in Atlantic City where we could be seen all dressed up. Mom packed several standup trunks for herself, my brother, and me. Excitement rose steadily until I was standing on the platform at Newark's Penn Station, covering my ears as the great electric locomotive swept by. We rode in a car with seats that swiveled like barbers' chairs, but mostly, I hung out with the porter in the vestibule between the cars. A porter once pointed to his own house as we passed through North Philadelphia.

At the Chalfonte-Haddon Hall we were early to breakfast: popovers served by a bus boy from a muffin warmer. My brother and I would then cruise the Boardwalk on rented bikes while Mom wrote long letters to her friends about the weather and the hotel events. Sometimes my brother and I would go to the DuPont exhibit to watch the working model of a rubber-making plant or to the Heinz theater pier to see free films about America's industrial might. Afternoons were spent with Mom in the auction galleries watching wiry black men lift enormous oriental rugs to the top of a giant parqueted easel, and then, when Mr. Brandt, the auctioneer, gave the signal, let the carpets unroll and slap down under brilliant lights. Mother once bought a large rug to impress the women's groups that met at our house. The rug covered the floor in the seldom-used living room where our dogs went to pee when they couldn't get outdoors in time.

A week in Atlantic City was like being in a movie. Dad appeared on the weekends. Dinner at Haddon Hall was a pageant. I knew well in advance what I would wear each night. I had to polish my shoes, keeping the polish off the top edges so it wouldn't rub off on my white socks, then I'd clip on a striped necktie with a huge Windsor knot. Mom dressed in a long dark green or maroon gown. In leather-soled shoes I was an electric generator as I crossed the carpet to leave our room. Sometimes a spark would jump three inches from my fingers to the brass door knob.

The pageant got moving in the hotel corridor en route to the dining room. Other guests would be leaving their rooms, and while waiting for an elevator, the adults made small talk. Their pleasantries occasionally developed into Christmas card exchanges, sometimes even visits.

At the entrance to the dining room we fell silent waiting our turn by family to be paraded down the broad blue carpet by a tuxedoed head waiter past an ice sculpture lit from below, past Corinthian columns surrounded by potted fishtail palms, past white-jacketed men carrying Sterno-fired bread warmers containing sticky buns, past aproned women carrying condiment trays. Waitresses and tray-laden busboys all paused in deference to us at the carpet's edge. Somewhere behind the palms played a spirited violin, cello, and piano. A head waiter held my mother's chair as she sat down and inched her forward to the table. Mom preferred the meat she ate broiled until blackened, and with great regularity she sent food back to the kitchen. So predictable was this routine that all she had to do was furrow her brow, and Dad or I would ask the waitress to return the steak or chops to the broiler until it was almost "incinerated" (a word I learned early and used often). Mom's eyes would dance in delight when the remains finally came to rest before her.

Once, when I was recovering from pneumonia at Haddon Hall, I was pushed in a wheelchair through the main kitchen past ovens where beef broth was skimmed off, just for me. Mother had Pop-Pop's vision of a grand style, and I, too, was all wrapped up in it.

At the end of the week Mom tipped the help. Bus boys and elevator men got two dollars, our waitress and room maid got seven dollars, and the head waiter, if he seated us at a prominent table, was slipped a five spot. The tip always changed hands with eye contact and never a downward glance. I was fascinated by head waiters. They seemed to have eyes in the back of their heads, for they could move sideways or backwards without looking to get out of the way of a guest or waitress. They moved as dancers.

In fourth grade I was enrolled in Miss Dotterer's dancing classes, known as Hobby Hall. In our town it was one way the children of "better-off" families were segregated from most of the rest of the kids. Parents' nominations of a few Italian and Armenian children were also accepted. Several children of poor families were given scholarships secretly, as were the children whose family fell upon hard times.

In the corner of an old ballroom behind an enormous Chickering grand piano, an aged woman rolled out a waltz or fox trot with an irresistible beat. For years we circled the floor counterclockwise under the eyes of the chaperones in long dresses, at first just holding hands, then in the traditional ballroom dancing position. Classmate Marilyn Hughes Johnson recalls:

> One of the things I remember is fingernail inspec-
> tion. The other thing is a lot of matching. You
> acquired a partner by matching cards that had been
> cut in half. In other words, if I got half of the eight
> of hearts, I would search for my partner and he
> would search for me because he would have the
> other half of the eight of hearts. I liked dancing
> school. I wasn't quite as good a dancer as some of
> my classmates, but it was a lot of fun.

In retrospect, Hobby Hall was the preëminent institution for teaching grooming habits and inculcating limits on social contacts. It continued my parents' sense of proper decorum and acceptable dating partners without their having to say a word. Mom was long embarrassed that when invited to chaperone a dance, she had mistakenly showed up in a short, rather than long, dress.

Mom was determined to avoid mistakes in guiding her boys to suitable mates. Dating, as distinct from dancing classes, also began in fourth grade with an afternoon "tea dance" sponsored by the Children of the American Revolution. One of the C.A.R. mothers drove me to an assigned classmate's home, where I presented a gardenia to the girl. We were then driven to the dance. Records were played; we circled the floor for an hour. Then, after graceless bows and curtsies, we disappeared with our respective parents.

When I got to the age of serious interest in girls, religion entered the list of standards. Relationships with Jews and Roman Catholics were out of bounds; girls of Protestant denominations other than our own were suspect. I was propelled toward Presbyterian young ladies.

The first girl I fell for passed the religion test, but her mother was termed "too common" by Mom. Unless a girlfriend demonstrated as much interest in my parents as in me, she was accused of being "out to get me." Mom was becoming a real pain in the ass: she would not tolerate her sons dating anyone she found fault with. But, ultimately, she had to.

Going out or coming in from dates was fraught with danger. Mom discussed with Dad within my hearing what she thought of the young women my brother dated and their families. Disapproval, and occasionally approval, of personal mannerisms, perceived discourtesies and the lack of outgoingness toward my parents, conversational ability, telephone etiquette, clothing styles, family occupations, dating locations, and the dependability of chaperones filled the air.

Lafayette Grisby, Jr., became a legend in Summit for his leadership in academics, athletics, and student government. I was in ninth grade when he graduated. I searched for him during his retirement years because I carried clear memories of his handyman father and knew of his fame. His late cousin Fatíma was my classmate.

Faith Stranad, the artist daughter of a sometimes cantankerous evangelical preacher, insisted that love could solve all problems, even my mom's. Her kitchen door was always open to me; her sunny disposition, a bright light in my world.

Good brother Put often had a different perspective on our parents' demands. Watching him deal with them helped me a lot. As the older child, he learned when to keep his mouth shut. At their wits' end with me, my parents sometimes consulted with him—and occasionally took his advice. Lucky for me!

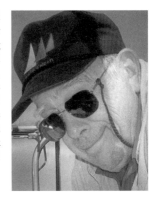

When Lafayette Grisby arrived at Colgate University, his roommates had already been asked if they "minded" rooming with a black man. Nobody asked Lafayette if he minded rooming with two white guys. Lafayette's philosopher dad set him up to enjoy learning and handle whatever came his way—or didn't, and that willingness helped propel him through Harvard University's Graduate School of Arts and Sciences and into the United States Information Agency as a Specialist on Eastern European Affairs.

As a leader-scholar-athlete and high school senior in nineteen fifty-one, Lafayette became the talk of white Summit parents who were accustomed to worrying about an entirely different range of situations. They simply couldn't imagine a black man without money or family connections attending one of their colleges. They were unprepared to acknowledge he was admitted on his own merit.

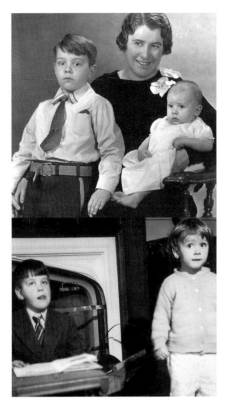

Whenever my brother was around, I spent time with him until he drove me away with his cap pistol. My dad's cousin Sybil dubbed us the Chinese brothers "Who Me?" and "Me Too!" It wasn't that I lacked ways to entertain myself (or others), rather, Put brought me a different world, and I liked to play in it—or take it apart. When he returned on his first leave from New York Military Academy, we built a rifle range in the basement together.

Dad's father, "W.F.," (second from left) performed in a trombone kazoo quartet with his Missouri Synod Lutheran buddies. "Formal" and "hijinx" describes these serious funsters. When Grandfather Putnam once overheard Dad lecturing my brother, he walked right on by, muttering, "Don't take it all out of him."

Dad picked up his parents' Czech-Austrian theatricality early. Evenings in the late eighteen-nineties, beneath the glow of a Welsbach mantle, Dad learned Lutheran hymns, mechanical drawing, and the fine points of jurisprudence.

Passage into adolescence included dismissal from the safety patrol for throwing a snowball at a car (a teacher's car: oops!) and stealing money from Mom. My classmates (shown in a photo I took in 6th grade) didn't understand my outlaw deeds, but Dad did, and while he didn't condone my behavior, he prevented Mom from dispatching me to reform school.

Samuel Putnams Hosts On 50th Anniversary

Brooklyn Couple Have Dinner for Relatives, Friends

Mr. and Mrs. Samuel Putnam, of 90 Eighth Avenue, Brooklyn, and Atlantic Highlands, N. J., gave a dinner last evening in the Perroquet Suite of the Waldorf-Astoria in celebration of their fiftieth wedding anniversary. Mrs. Putnam wore her wedding gown of old-ivory satin and point lace in which she was married on Oct. 26, 1892, in Brooklyn. She is the former Miss Mary Elizabeth Nugent, daughter of the late Brigadier General Robert Nugent, U. S. A., and the late Mrs. Nugent. She was born at Fort Douglass, Salt Lake City. Mr. Putnam was born in New York and is president of Putnam & Co.

Among the guests were the couple's son-in-law and daughter, Mr. and Mrs. John C. Brodsky, of Summit, N. J., and their children, J. Putnam

The Brooklyn Scotch-Irish, Germans, and Dutch men were engineers, manufacturers, physicians and attorneys. Many of the women were professionals, too. They went to great lengths to impress one another at formal dinners. Multiple tables would have been tacky. Days were devoted to planning the invitation list and seating arrangement. Day-after press releases were written. Pop-Pop and Nanny's 50th wedding anniversary celebration set a standard in our family.

Mom's annual visit to a grand hotel in Atlantic City was one way she maintained her image among "the better class of people." My brother and I found plenty of amusements and a joke shop that had nothing to do with being around "a better class."

However far we ranged along the Boardwalk, from the Heinz industrial movie theatre to the Convention Hall, or whether we were hiding out with the hotel bellmen or game room attendant, we were careful to anticipate Mom's concerns. Before the hotels were commandeered as military hospitals during the Second World War, I was marched each afternoon to a "health bar" on the mezzanine to gag down strange vegetable concoctions.

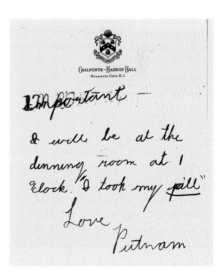

Paradiddles

—EVEN BEATS, YET DIFFERENT

Right, left, right, right; left, right, left, left, continuing in the same pattern. The paradiddle is a drumming rudiment written like four eighth or sixteenth notes, but it doesn't sound quite like that. Something is different about the beats: the last two are struck with the same hand. Try it with your fingers on the edge of a table, gradually increasing the speed. Can you hear the difference? I'm not sure my parents could; they were so absorbed in their own rudiments. But paradiddles in combination with other rudiments fill drumming with variations that give the listener a curious combination of secure repetition and new phrasing.

Mom and Dad were so predictable in their beliefs and practices that I learned to self-censor mine when in their presence. Yet, at an early age, I noticed there were other rudiments beside Mom and Dad's. There were different beats to listen to, and these beats caught my attention. They happened when we went to different places and when other people entered my life. They were interesting; they were fun; they were important.

Summer Escapes

The neighborhood around Pop-Pop's summer place in Leonardo, New Jersey, was very different from my suburban home town. To begin with, the road alongside our summer house was surfaced with bankrun gravel. After a cloudburst, the appearance of the road grader brought a day's excitement. Down that road by the beach stood the blind soldiers' home, a Spanish-American War Gatling gun on the front lawn pointing at visitors. The cottage owners along the beach of Sandy Hook Bay would yell at us when we walked our dog in front of their porches. And next to our driveway was the home of a kindly retired railroad crossing gate attendant and his wife. The Marigolds rented their house for the summer and moved to a little green cabin in the grove out back where Mrs. M. continued her sewing business. Mr. M. would pause whatever he was doing when I appeared by his fence and take the occasion to repack his pipe with Prince Albert while we talked. I liked to watch him sharpen his ball-bearing lawnmower and chop weeds in his garden.

Pop-Pop and Dad commuted to Manhattan aboard the excursion boat "Sandy Hook," and Pop-Pop's chauffeur, Arthur Dillard, and the Swedish cook, Louise Jacobsen, looked after his summer place and the rest of us. I helped Louise preserve pears and squeeze grapes and apples through cheesecloth for jelly. Louise rewarded me with chocolate butter-and-sugar-iced cakes. I hung out at the garage with Arthur and learned to love the smell of the Murphy's Oil Soap he used to wash the cars.

Pop-Pop had a screened-in sandbox built by the house, and my brother set up an oiled canvas tent in the wooded lot next door. But the best summer playground was the Isaksens' yard, down toward the water. The Isaksens were Norwegian fishermen and clammers, and there were a lot of them. Their yard was filled with rust-covered fishing gear and a decaying car, heavenly terrain for kids. The older Isaksens knew about all the junk and welcomed the summer kids.

With the coming of WWII the scrap metal disappeared, and even with the shared experience of victory gardens, Mom gradually drew us away from the Isaksens by scheduling other events for us. She made sure some of our parties got reported in the society columns.

In spite of gas rationing, my grandfather managed to find an adequate supply so Arthur could drive us to a private beach club ten miles away almost every day. While Arthur, in black uniform, snoozed in the hot sun in the black leather cab of the black limousine, Mom fretted over the rambunctious teenagers of Irish Catholic families frolicking around the pool.

Dad had spent summers on the Adirondack lakes with college classmates, and soon my parents introduced me to the New England forests and the saw mills that sprang up after the 1938 hurricane devastated them. When my brother turned 13, he was packed off to a camp in Vermont. He left on the camp train from New York, but Mom, Dad, and I soon followed.

In midsummer we arrived at a rustic cabin colony near the camp. From our porch I could hear campers shrieking in delight. I don't recall ever having heard such sounds of joy before—either on the school playground or at the beach club. So, the following winter, I lobbied hard to be sent to camp, too. Although I was only eight, I was successful, and I never became homesick.

Camp was a new universe for me. The north, east and south sides of the camp were bordered by a lake and other camps, but the west side disappeared into deep woods, beyond which, we were warned, were only bears and tramps; the very thought of either raised goose bumps. The five summers I spent at Camp Passumpsic were full of discoveries: a meteorite too heavy to lift, salamanders prowling under rocks, going out on overnight trips and sleeping on the ground in the rain. I watched a snapping turtle lunge toward an incautious counselor. We sang together every day. I capsized a sailboat in a sudden squall far out on the lake. Around a weekly council fire, where no parent could either approve or disapprove, we talked of these things. Then, in silence, we pondered ashes from previous years' fires dug up and added to the flames. Over the glowing coals a counselor would read us a good story.

I never felt ashamed while at camp, except once, when I reported in great excitement that I had seen two rocks growing together under a waterfall. The camp director calmly responded that just maybe a single rock was being worn by the water into two pieces.

Mom and Dad rented a nearby cottage again for half the summer and let the camp director's wife know their displeasure in discovering a mess in my cabin. Mrs. Starry looked me straight in the eye, and without trace of malice said, "Well, I guess the camp mother will have to check up on Cabin 5." That was the last I heard of the matter. Dad liked my second counselor, John Lidstone, a Canadian painter and art teacher, perhaps because, like my father, he could draw a straight line freehand. I liked Mr. Lidstone, too. He taught me to look for subtle hues in the light shining on a white birch trunk and paint them with watercolors.

Our days were ordered by the bugle. We began each day at the flagpole. As members of either the red or gray team we competed against one another, even in singing. We learned how to start a fire when all the wood was wet, how to make a canoe track straight in a cross wind, and how to handle a rifle. There was a craft shop where we could make almost anything we could imagine and build in ten hours.

Also, a photo darkroom, where I made an enlargement of Mr. Starry flipping flapjacks. Everyone learned to swim, to dive deep, and to tread water for five minutes. All achievements were recognized through a system of awards. Sunday evenings a nonsectarian God was honored from a grove above the lake to the accompaniment of a portable reed organ and symphonic chimes.

When WWII ended, ex-G.I.'s appeared as counselors, armed with dirty jokes, dirty songs and tales of sex. Strains of "One-Ball Riley" replaced "The Road to Mandalay" and "On the Oregon Trail." Hormones raged, at least until I got home and the dutiful son reëmerged.

Five summers of Vermont camping ended when Pop-Pop got sick. I was twelve. During his months of illness, Mom visited him daily in Manhattan, while I became a latchkey kid, accomplished at preparing frozen dinners. I tired of these and began cooking for myself; camp experience was paying off.

When Pop-Pop died, Mom forced her mother out of Brooklyn and winterized the summer house. I spent my thirteenth summer stringing telephone cable between summer houses and scraping and painting porch ceilings to the accompaniment of Red Barber and the Brooklyn Dodgers from the radio. The following winter a classmate invited me and my parents to his home to meet the leader of a Southwestern mobile camp. Once again I was able to step away from my family.

Unlike the Vermont camp, the Southwestern trek asked us to read about where we were going, then pursue an area of science or art, such as archeology, mineralogy, herpetology, spelunking or photography. We were expected to keep a notebook and to submit a report after we returned home. I made photo books and a sound-slide show.

The daily routine of the expedition was mundane: we became

filling station sanitation experts and the world's fastest tire changers. When our cook burned his stomach swigging down a bottle of vinegar on a wager, I assumed his duties and got invited back a second summer to cook and keep track of supplies.

One morning I ignorantly substituted baking soda for baking powder in a coffee cake. At 8000' it still rose impressively, but soon the air was filled with loud sounds of spitting. To my surprise, everyone took it as a big joke. There were also times of real terror, such as when I crawled alone deep into a narrow cave to retrieve a lost hunting knife that slipped from its sheath on my first exploration, and again when the pre-historic handholds on a cliff face ran out at twilight and I was only halfway to the top. In the gloaming I inched back down. When my beard began to grow and I decided to buy a razor, I approached a store clerk with the improbable line, "Left my double-edge back East." She smiled.

We learned to sit a horse and respect Native Americans. A Navajo pharmacy student, Narcisco Abeyta, came to live with us for a while. Where he ran, we huffed. We visited hogons and pueblos. When we tried to dig a channel for a stranded ferry to cross the Colorado, the river made fools of us.

I almost forgot about Mom and Dad, but Mom and Dad didn't forget me. I could hear Mom's rant over my less-than-expected flow of letters behind Dad's calm wording of the telegram he sent me. Mom later said that allowing me to go out West was the greatest mistake she made with me. But she said this about other things, too.

Sally Hansen

A child of Polish immigrants whose family acquired a Scandinavian name, Sally Hansen was impressive in her stiff blue and white nurse's cap. But her whooping laugh could take the starch out of anyone's habit. When recounting how our springer spaniel hid under the bed, then emerged to bite Dr. Bullwinkle after he gave my brother a painful shot, Sally could reach a crescendo heard out on the street. Sally was around when I was an infant, nursed each of us when we were really sick or in the hospital, and stayed in touch during the war years between trips across the Atlantic and Pacific tending to the wounded. From her giant hand bag weighed down with a Physicians' Desk Reference protruded the *New York Daily News* and a current racing sheet, both of which she read to me. While lying in a hospital bed, I could usually hear Sally precede herself out of the elevator. Sally was known as much for saving doctors' reputations as for drinking them under the table.

"What a stinker your Mom could be," Sally told me. Mom once drove Sally to walk out. When Dad arrived home, he called Sally and sweet-talked her into returning to work, promising to put the kibosh on further interference from Mom.

"You know," Sally told me from her nursing home bed, "your mom could also go far out of her way to be nice to me and my friends. When I visited your folks in Florida with two girl friends, she put us up for an entire week in her apartment. And we had the best of times together." Other people had a similar experience with my mom.

Genevieve Hayes

Mom's sense of family duty required her to invite her two cousins on holidays and for a week at the summer house, and their housemate, Genevieve, came along, too. One of Mom's cousins was a secretary for my grandfather, the other kept house, but Aunt Genevieve, as I was taught to call her, was a Manhattan public school principal. Genevieve Hayes shared a similar body build with my mother, but the resemblance stopped there. Genevieve was a spirited defender of contemporary Catholicism and also had an addiction to *The New York Times*. For me she always had a twinkle in her eye, but my mom held public schools suspect, vocally abhorred Catholicism, and scorned *The New York Times*.

During "the girls' visit," as my father would refer to it, *The New York Times* was delivered to our house and often displayed across Aunt Genevieve's wide lap. "Look at this," she'd say, baiting Mom, and then proceed to read an article so public-spirited even Mom couldn't take issue. Mom would react by disappearing into the kitchen.

Seldom a day would pass without Mom finding something to take exception to in Catholic belief or behavior, such as the mediating role of the priesthood or the authority of the pope. The cousins would deflect Mom's attacks with an "Oh, Dorothy, you can't really mean that." Mom, knowing she was outgunned, would again retreat into the kitchen as one of them shot a wink in my direction. Some nights, long after bedtime, I would lie on the threadbare carpet at the top of the stairs, listening to their discussions. In the morning a cheery Aunt Genevieve would greet me with a big wet smooch, and again read something inspiring from *The New York Times* while Mom would huff about.

Mr. Berkelhammer

Near the center of Summit stood Maple Hardware and Paint— an interesting store, filled with lots of stuff, and presided over by an interesting proprietor, Mr. Berkelhammer. Of course, I knew he was a Jew; Mom had seen to it that I acquired the requisite antennae. A cautionary bell rang in my brain. But when I'd drop in to buy sandpaper or paint or friction tape, Mr. Berkelhammer would come out from behind the counter and with a show of genuine interest ask what I was up to and how my family were getting on. Then he would tell me about his son Gerry and his studies toward a career in medicine. Mr. Berkelhammer was filled with excitement for us all. The prejudicial ringing in my brain was being dulled by Mr. Berkelhammer's interest and actions. His store became a kind of holy ground for me. I loved to go there.

Joe Stranad

As I entered adolescence and began to challenge my family's values, Mom sought counsel and comfort from Faith, the young artist next door. Faith radiated warmth; her husband, Joe, was the neighborhood blow torch. Joe's day job was to assist the president of the National Lead Company, but his consolation was art. As an amateur photographer, he'd studied under the renowned printmaker of The New York Photo League, Ghislain Lootens. Lootens' book became my bible as Joe guided my passion for photography.

When Joe told my parents to buy me a simple folding camera and a Brownie Darkroom Kit, they did, and I disappeared with the kit into the basement toilet. Another neighbor soon invited me to use his luxurious darkroom and his press camera. Joe's roots, like mine, were in Czechoslovakia, and together we studied classical European composition and printing technique. I began to look at everything as through a frame. When I brought him my best darkroom effort, Joe once said, "Bobby, there is no real black in this print. I want to see a black somewhere in every print, a black that is so black there is nothing there, not even black paper. I want to see a black so black it reflects no light, do you hear what I'm saying?—like a hole that goes all the way to Hell. Now, bring me a print that tells me you've gone to Hell." Sufficiently traumatized,

I scurried off into the darkness to attempt a better print. When, at fifteen, I finally produced a print that met Joe's definition of black, he found more things to praise me for. I had learned to manipulate the gray scale in exposing and developing prints as well as negatives. Faith, his wife, noticed other things:

> Joe and Bob had so much in common. I didn't always know what it was, but most of it would be about photography. Earnestly going into details and cameras and the new equipment and how to turn one in that was not quite up to snuff and get another one because they'd take them in like cars.... And it was the most wonderful, satisfactory thing to Joe because Bob knew what he was talking about. He really liked to be with Bob.

My craft in photography led to paying projects all over town and beyond. Without asking, I took black & white photos of the big homes in springtime, using a red filter to make the sky very dark behind the clouds and dogwood blossoms. When I rang their door bells with a large print in a deckle-edge folder and asked for two dollars, the homeowners suspected I was a shill for my father. But they soon learned I was for real, and I was invited to photograph business establishments, dogs for kennel shows and exclusive club events in places my parents had never been, such as trade shows in New York. Much praise fell upon Mom and Dad because of my work, and the income from the projects paid for all the photo experiments I could dream up. I was no longer tempted to steal.

But more than economic independence, photography began to teach me about the world and myself. I learned to estimate projects.

I learned I could be fooled. And I learned a visual language: I learned the dynamics of graphic arts, I worked with my darkroom easel to adjust compositions, and I intentionally made prints that were too dark so I could later selectively bring out highlights with Farmer's reducer on a cotton swab or retouching brush.

And then, when I entered high school, it suddenly ended.

Danny's Room

When Nanny died, Mom inherited enough money to move to the society town of her childhood dreams on the north New Jersey shore. Implicit in this was the call for me to put photography aside and decide upon a suitable career for myself—suitable to my parents, that is. In ninth grade social studies I had to create a booklet on a vocation that interested me. I did mine on illustrative photography, or how to make good photographs of everything but people. A dramatic montage cover opened upon samples of my work and a homage to photographers I admired, such as Victor Keppler and Aubrey Bodine. I got a high mark, except from Mom and Dad, who were distressed that I had allowed Latin and math to slide.

In Mom's new hometown my parents took me to visit the school superintendent, and he told us flat out that I should not go to his high school if they wanted me to attend an Ivy League college, as my brother was doing. So they took me to Lawrenceville School. There, the sight of future leaders of the free world trooping out of their field house in sport jackets with rep ties blowing in the breeze made me dizzy. I was in free-fall.

My brother's fiancée, Peggy Morse, whose family lived around the corner from us in Summit, tried to calm my rising anxiety. "Don't worry," she said, "the friends you'll keep will be your college friends."

But seeing my continuing distress, she asked her parents to allow me to live in the room recently left vacant by the death of her grandmother, Mrs. Daniels, so I could finish high school with my present friends and school activities. Within a week they offered to board me if my parents consented and if the high school would keep me as a tuition student. I went into high gear negotiations with Mom and Dad, and Principal A.J. Bartholomew said, "O.K."

The Morse family had another boarder, a Bell Labs intern, Wally Walker, recently discharged from the Navy. Late in the evening, Peggy, Wally and I would gather around the battered zinc-covered kitchen table to talk about everything while Mother Morse made soup from leftover oatmeal and table scraps. To send their two daughters to private school and Smith College, tiny Mother Morse became an expert in frugality. She would scrape a bone until it looked as though it had been bleached in the sun. I called her nightly production "battleship soup" because it was always the color of naval camouflage. The flavor was good, and it made you feel ready to conquer the seven seas. After the three of us turned in, Mother Morse would go to work on the linoleum floor with beeswax softened in turpentine. Her daytime passion was talking to her friends on the telephone, holding court from a chair in a dark hallway leading to the powder room.

She was Episcopalian, the faith of her turn-of-the-century naval officer father. Her husband, Robert, although educated in parochial boarding schools while his mining engineer father toured the globe, had become an amiable agnostic. He entered M.I.T. at fifteen, a prototypical geek. He had two passions: underground electrical cable and Gilbert & Sullivan operettas, either of which he could hold forth upon when I sat with him in his study.

Mother Morse hoarded rags to send to the Olson Rug Co., which would exchange them for hooked rugs. But their home was also furnished with inherited oriental carpets and valuable antiques, including a large Steinway piano, which I was encouraged to play.

When they gave gifts, which they were doing constantly, they either ordered from Tiffany's or, if something practical seemed appropriate, went to the hardware store. On my birthdays they gave me elegant metal waste baskets, twice. For a wedding present they gave me a vacuum cleaner; we laughed a lot. It didn't matter that their clothing seemed to come out of their parents' closets.

Living with the Morses was a step up in WASPdom. Where my mother was D.A.R, Mrs. Morse was a Colonial Dame. The Morse family were as secure in their social position as my mother wasn't. They had what they wanted, did what they wanted, and were wracked with ordinary Puritan social anxieties, as distinct from my family's tempests, which grew out of Victorian ambition. I had simply jumped from one soup pot into another, and the latter didn't bubble quite so violently.

During my junior year Mother Morse asked me if I'd like to invite some friends to supper before the Junior Prom. I did, and four couples were formally invited. Then I wrote my parents about it, and as soon as they got my note they telephoned to say, "Cancel the party." They said I was inconsiderate not to consult them first and ungrateful for all they were trying to do for me. I was so embarrassed I went to see my school guidance counselor and broke down in front of her. I acknowledged being neglectful of my parents' feelings, but I was loathe to retract the invitations. She came down on my parents' side and left me feeling inconsiderate, ungrateful, and now, emotionally unstable. I canceled the party.

The Reverend Leonard V. Buschman, D.D.

In late winter of my senior year at Summit High, Dr. Buschman, the silver-haired avuncular pastor of Central Presbyterian, sent for me. I had never before been inside his private study, and I was surprised by its austere furnishings: only a small desk, a glass-front bookcase, and three wooden chairs. He greeted me warmly, then took a seat by the light of a window to which he held what looked like a letter. He said he'd received it from a man he thought I knew quite well and wanted to see how I reacted. It was from Joe Stranad, my old photography coach. "He's just been elected to our Board of Deacons," Dr. Buschman began. "He wrote me this, and I don't know what to make of it." Dr. Buschman then read me Joe's thoroughly damning judgment of Dr. Buschman's preaching. I remember the letter closed to the effect that, "You are a disciple of the devil and have no right to be in the pulpit of any church." I was scandalized, but more than that, I felt that Dr. Buschman was looking for something from me to help him grapple with this problem. I was a leader in Central Presbyterian's Youth Fellowship. I was expected to say something clear and insightful.

I knew how stern and forceful Joe could be from the days he taught me to compose photos with great intentionality and make impressive prints, but I hadn't talked with Joe since my folks had moved out of town; photography was three years behind me. His attack sounded religious, and I was not equipped to see its base in politics.

In those years one issue dominated American politics: fighting Communism. One day while helping Mom turn mattresses, a cigarette tightly clenched in her mouth, we listened to a live radio broadcast of the House Un-American Activities Committee hearings. Mom was addicted to political commentary, and she was all for punishing those who opposed the good judgments of businessmen. When we bought a sailboat for cheap from a blacklisted radio announcer, I felt fortunate to be on the side of good judgments. Growing up Republican, I was deaf to the crippling crusade of Senator Joseph McCarthy.

I later learned Joe was accusing Dr. Buschman of being soft on Communism because he spoke out against the destructive influence of McCarthyism.

It wasn't because Dr. Buschman was a clergyman, per se, that he advocated abandonment of the loyalty oaths that were being demanded by government, business, civic and educational authorities. Most clergymen were either silent on these matters or in full support of them. Protestant clergymen had long been in the forefront of credalism that routinely called for weekly professions of beliefs during worship services.

But Dr. Buschman was among those teaching elders who were in touch with the Calvinist universities both in Scotland and on the European continent. In 1933, when Hitler was selected to lead Germany out of the ruins of The Great War, he immediately attempted to bring church youth groups under his control. Roman Catholics and Calvinist Protestants proved difficult to persuade. Protestant leaders gathered in the little town of Barmen to clarify where they stood. Their meeting yielded a document proclaiming God alone as they knew him through the scriptures of the Christian church and through the preaching of their duly ordained ministers as the final authority for church members. Hitler may have gotten their vote, but not their loyalty. The authors of the Barmen Declaration were gradually quarantined. Some were imprisoned; some were murdered by their neighbors and the authorities. As a trustee of Princeton Theological Seminary, Dr. Buschman was familiar with the events that led educated people to gradually accept fascism, and he knew the cost of failing to speak out against it.

Within sight of my bedroom window with the Morse family lived Dr. Glenn Moore, who, along with Dr. John Mackay, the worldly-wise scholar-president of Princeton Theological Seminary, was a senior officer of the Presbyterian Church in the U.S.A. As Senator McCarthy used live radio to raise suspicions of Communist sympathies among religious leaders, Mackay and Moore worked together to publish "A Letter to Presbyterians" asking church members to stay the course and resist the national hysteria. The document caused great controversy.

In the early nineteen-nineties, when I went looking for materials related to "A Letter to Presbyterians" and the Barmen Declaration in Princeton's Speer and Firestone libraries, I was surprised to find only a few references in English. Now, however, these and other church documents making the case for humility and tolerance are being studied, debated, and honored.

I have no recollection of what I said to Dr. Buschman that day, but I know I was very troubled to hear Joe's letter. It was becoming quite a year for me. I recognized in that attack the clear, strong voice that had trained me in photographic technique. But the loudest voices in my own life at that moment were those of my parents, pressing me to declare a career path for myself. There wasn't even much time for girls, though I did sneak out to the burlesque halls of Newark with other guys.

When I left Dr. Buschman's office, I experienced a flood of emotion that resulted a few weeks later in my decision to become a minister. I guess I saw a career in the ministry as a place of authority from which I could move people to make peace instead of war. At the time, I thought the Stranad/Buschman conflict was primarily personal. I didn't understand the political context.

Pop-Pop's cook and housekeeper, Louise Jacobsen, and his chauffeur, Arthur Dillard, put me to "work" with them. Arthur let me play in the limousine and make things at his tool bench. Louise made me help with canning and preserving fruit. Both servants died in my grandfather's service, Arthur, in the car at the curb. They taught me to enjoy work.

Never underestimate the ingenuity and energy of a Norwegian band. The Isaksens, old and young, were great kids to play with, especially in their yard.

The odor of an oiled tent hinted at liberation from the family regime, but sometimes adults invaded the wood lot to stage birthday parties. Afterward, the table and chairs would depart with the adults, and we would be left with the trees, the sandy clay, and the old army cots.

No one combined raucous laughter and informed medical practice better than nurse Sally Hansen. Mom could not dominate her and grew to truly respect her as a person.

Sally the Spaniel bit Dr. Bullwinkle after he gave my brother an injection. Sally Hansen was present and expressed nothing but praise for her namesake as she dressed the doctor's wound.

Neckties, tea dresses, and a notice on the society page. The compleat birthday party.

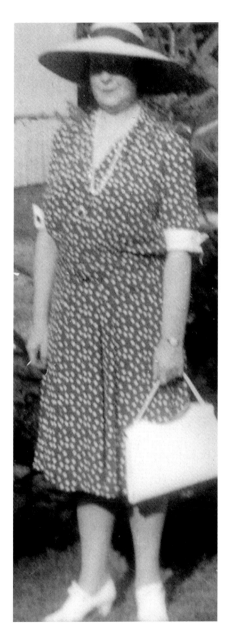

Manhattan school principal
Genevieve Hayes brought a
fresh understanding of the
responsibilities of democracy
and a civil state to our
Republican home. She accompanied her roommates, Mom's
cousins, Marnie and Irene
Nugent on summer visits.

Marnie and Irene ignored the
scorn Mom heaped on Irish
Roman Catholics. Mom located
her heritage among the
Presbyterian Scots though her
grandfather emigrated from
County Down, Ireland.

School teacher David Starry founded a boys camp in Vermont before the First World War. Twenty-five years later he was a paragon of "muscular Christianity," having built an impressive facility and gathered a competent staff. On an overnight trip to his nearby farm, I photographed him lofting French toast. Chief Starry presided at the Saturday evening council fires—evenings filled with stories, mysteries, and games. Charcoal from council fires past was added to the summer's first fire. All fires were lit by flint on steel.

The two summers I was able to spend in the Four Corners region of the Southwest pushed me into different cultures. At camp in Vermont, I had never met anyone like Navajo pharmacy student Narcisco Abeyta. He arrived on his own clock, left by it, and in between led us in Native American ways. Unlike Anglo ranchers, he was a flashy dresser.

When the auto-propelled ferry stranded on a sandbar in the Colorado River at Hite, Utah, we tried to dig a channel to get our caravan across. We failed. Geology students in our group took soundings and made a chart. I made a photo record of the event.

Maple Hardware was a source of things necessary to my imagination. I went there to buy sandpaper to finish a flower box I was making for Mom. When I was building my photo studio, the proprietor helped me find the right parts for a lighting distribution box.

Next-door neighbor Joe Stranad's house was built on rock, like his coaching about visual images. He made gardens around both. He spent many hours screening soil next to our hedge. I would wander over, and we'd talk photography and photographers. He also told me "the European formula for a happy marriage: a man should marry a woman one-half his age plus seven." I felt a bit scandalized he would talk to a twelve year old about such things.

Mr. Berkelhammer dispensed curiosity and kindness as well as hardware, wallpaper, and window glass from his store in the middle of Summit. He made a point of stopping sales and asking questions. He remembered the names of customers' children and their activities. The talk was always good.

Joe Stranad advised my dad on what photo equipment to buy to get me started, and soon I was developing film and contact printing pictures in a dark corner of the cellar. Seeing my earliest work, another neighbor invited me to use his darkroom and Speed Graphic. Photographing homes led to paying work with dogs of a kennel club breeder. I studied lighting and filters and print toning and hand coloring.

Pop-Pop wasn't well when I took his picture on a Sunday visit, but he was patient as I adjusted my lights and folding camera. He smoked fragrant "Between the Acts," little cigars that came in a small flat metal box and eventually affected his lungs. He sold the rolling ladder company he founded to two G.I.'s, who ran it well throughout their lives. The company has found new markets, and the employees—newer immigrants—are alive in the heritage.

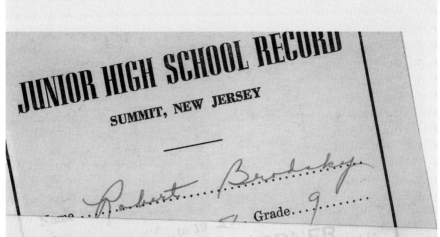

JUNIOR HIGH SCHOOL RECORD

SUMMIT, NEW JERSEY

Name ... *Robert Brodsky* ... Grade ... 9 ...

Robert's work as reflected on 3rd Report does not satisfy me. The cause may be not enough plugging in his studies and too much extra curricular activity; if so, I will encourage the home working (though considerable time is devoted to it now) and discourage some of the outside activities. The final J. H. year seems to me to require emphasis on studies, and calls for a commendable report.

The marking on personal and social habits looks a bit perfunctory to me.

Suggestions toward improving Bob's standing will be welcome.

John R. Murthy

My brother's fiancée, Peggy Morse, who lived a block away, spoke up for me when my parents, who had moved to another town, tried to send me away to a prep school. She asked her parents to offer me room and board while I finished high school. They took me in, and together with another boarder—a visiting Bell Labs engineer—we had wonderful times.

I found the Morse family a more tolerant household than Mom and Dad's. Although the families remained friendly, my parents strained the relationship when they tried to supervise me from afar.

PHOTO BY RON RICE

Used by permission of Princeton Theological Seminary

Dr. John Mackay, president of Princeton Theological Seminary. Under a formidable Scottish scholar lay a practical humanitarian. With my Summit neighbor, Dr. Glenn Moore, Secretary of the Presbyterian Church (U.S.A.), Mackay wrote "A Letter to Presbyterians," denouncing McCarthyism as well as Communism. My pastor, Dr. Buschman, was demonized by my former photo mentor Joe Stranad for encouraging the assistant pastor to sermonize on "A Letter...."

Dr. Buschman (lower right) enjoyed his seminary trusteeship, but the leaderships' stand against McCarthyism put him at odds with some members of his congregation.

Used by permission of Princeton Theological Seminary

If his Summit neighbors knew of his tolerant politics, Dr. Moore (here reading "A Letter to Presbyterians" to the General Council of the General Assembly) would have been pilloried, too. His daughter, Marilyn, was my classmate.

Used by permission of Presbyterian Historical Society, Presbyterian Church (U.S.A.) (Philadelphia)

71

Syncopations
—DISRUPTIONS THAT AFFECT YOUR BREATHING

Apart from members of my immediate family, there have been five people I can't stop thinking about. They are unlike my parents, and they are unlike the other people who introduced me to different street beats. In the Preface I called them the Others. They are like syncopations, rhythmic surprises, because their actions were so different from those I was accustomed to. The rhythms of life they presented me with ranged from significant hiccups to the life-threatening moments you may experience when running upstairs and your foot misses a tread. The things these people did also informed me that my life could be different—more in tune with my inclinations and less obedient to what others expected of me. They informed me that my life should be different because I was different from my parents.

Sara Sykora, Phi Beta Kappa

CoCo, as I called her when I began to speak, was my governess (as Mom referred to her) until I was almost five. She came to live with relatives after completing college in the Midwest and found a job with my mom, running after me. Mom hired her to keep track of me while she was attending to my brother during an extended bout with undulant fever. Brother Put remembered,

> She was somebody who was always there. A person
> who was very kind. She was somebody that I could
> go to in trouble. She was there to play games with,
> to read with. I don't specifically remember that she
> helped me with homework. She was a nice person.
> She was part of the family. She was there all of
> those years.

I remember the evening CoCo discovered I had a hernia. I was three and had been rearranging the living room furniture, dragging a large hassock around from one chair to another. CoCo was drying me after a bath with a large towel as I stood on a toilet seat and we both noticed the bump in my groin. CoCo showed no alarm but simply said Mom would take me to the doctor to have it fixed. CoCo inspired trust.

Coco was also an authority. She refereed play with neighborhood kids, organized exciting backyard circuses, and led impromptu parades. Sunday mornings I tagged along as Dad drove CoCo to Oaks Memorial Methodist Church. CoCo was just fun to be with. Her niece, Sally Hoffman, mused about growing up with CoCo in her childhood home:

> Sara would take walks in the woods with us, and
> maybe because she was a trained teacher, if she saw
> a dog-toothed violet, you had to stop and look at it,
> and she'd tell you about the dog-toothed violet.
> Or if you saw a skunk, you got a lot of information
> about the skunk. It was like, 'I can't help myself.'

Here is this opportunity and a raw mind, so I have to do something with it. But you never minded, because Sara was enjoying herself, and that was part of the key to the relationship.

If the person that you're with is enjoying what they're doing, you feel very comfortable with them. You always felt very comfortable with her and you knew that she loved you; you knew that regardless of what you did, you were a loved person. I think my brother probably felt that, too, with Sara, because it wasn't just me.

She would take us into New York City and take us to one of the big museums, like the Museum of New York City. She would spend time just doing a jigsaw puzzle with us, and these became great opportunities to pick up things from a person when you're doing something that informal. You're working on a jigsaw puzzle, but there are little bits of conversation going on at the same time. And it's out of these little bits of conversation that a sense of love comes across. Looking for a piece, and turning it around. You never felt like you were stumbling along, you felt like you were traveling the same road, almost at the same speed that she was. And yet that couldn't be possible because you were a child and Sara was light years ahead of you because of her keen intellect, being older, having had the education, having lived that much farther.

But you didn't know that. I didn't know it as a
child, but I know it now.

I was very blessed and very fortunate to have
had Sara single, a single woman, who loved, who
was there and added a dimension to my life.

About ten years ago I learned of the extent to which CoCo
stood up to Mom's bullying. My sister-in-law, Peggy, gave me an
envelope of 3 x 5 slips of paper cryptically labeled in Mom's hand-
writing, "For Miss Sykora, to read sometime:"

My dear Mrs. Brodsky: you seem to be so busy
concentrating on your present cook's [Hilma's] 'bad'
points that it might be well for someone to point
out to you a few of her [good] ones —
1. She is really clean.
2. She is good-natured.
3. She keeps the entire house quite clean besides
    doing <u>all</u> the cooking and the family wash.
4. She cleans all the silverware oftener than anyone
    else you've had.
5. She cleans the bathrooms twice a week.
6. She feeds the dogs entirely and prepares their
    food 2-3 times a week.
7. She is good to but does not spoil the children.
8. She is grateful for assistance.
9. She is not extravagant.

You complained before that the help <u>did</u> <u>not</u> do these things and you still seem only to find fault. Maybe you do not <u>know</u> you are doing it or maybe you do not realize how good Hilma is since you are not home as much as I am. Perhaps these little notes will set you right. I hope so as you have seemed most unfair in your judgment. I cannot stand unfairness.

CoCo

P.S. I forgot to mention how much better the kitchen, stove, pots & pans are cared for.

Did my mom, in writing, "For Miss Sykora, to read sometime," think CoCo would repent of what she had written? (Did CoCo think my mom would be "set right" by this list?) CoCo wrote this during the depths of the Great Depression when jobs were hard to come by, especially for women, even for a Phi Beta Kappa woman. She was probably fired for expressing her feelings. I was present when Mom fired other employees for less outspokenness. I remember Dad taking me to visit CoCo at her relatives' home a few miles away after CoCo had found work in the Bell Labs offices.

CoCo faced me with a regard not present elsewhere in my family. While Mom sought social advantages for her boys, and Dad gently lectured us on proper deportment, CoCo was infusing us with self-respect. And that self-respect manifested itself early on in tremendous excitement over the world around me. I learned it was O.K. to think about things, and then to relate things to one another, and later to synthesize ideas and compare events. I've never been bored (although I've been afraid of lots of things and mourned lots of things). I've been depressed, but I've never been bored. And because of the head start CoCo gave me, I've been able to gain control of most of my fears, I've been able to limit mourning, and my episodes of moodiness have passed rather quickly.

Every day, just by being who she was, CoCo enabled me to think of myself a little differently. I was not only a child who, as my mother too often put it, "could drive a saint to distraction," I was a person who could confidently investigate things, make decisions, and do things. CoCo's note says it all; it must have blown Mom away.

Miss Edna A. Brandenburg

"Old Brandywine" was the nickname we gave the formidable principal of Brayton Elementary School, formidable in her directness and her wisdom. When I, along with two other boys, was bothering fifth grade classmate Margie Romach, there was trouble. Margie had irresistibly long pigtails, and when we played with them, she complained to our teacher, who informed the principal. Miss Brandenburg summoned all four of us to her office, where, stepping out from behind her desk to a personal distance much too close for comfort to us boys, she looked over at Margie and said, "You know, Marjorie, when boys bother you, it really means they *like* you." The temperature in the tiny office rose ten degrees before Miss Brandenburg shooed us back to class. The harassment ceased.

Miss B. would whisk into our classroom with a much-traveled tomato basket on her arm containing arithmetic tests purpled by a spirit duplicator. The episodes were quick and challenging, but bore no enduring pain. On longer visits she led animated spelling bees. Outside of the classrooms, she worked with families to overcome their racism. Neighbor and parent Faith Stranad remembered:

> Edna Brandenburg knew that I had graduated from Gulf Park College in Louisiana, sixty miles from New Orleans. And that I was prejudiced because of the way that people in Louisiana think and do what they do with the black people. Edna Brandenburg knew all about it; we all told her everything. She was just that kind of a person who listens to everything and cares because you have children there. And she said to me, 'Faith, would you please do the yearbook this year?—all of the illustrations for the miscellaneous things that are not A, B, Cs.' And I said, 'Well, I'm awfully busy.' And she said, 'Faith, I haven't got anyone else this year who is an artist or who will sit and do it and finish it.' And I said, 'All right, I'll do it, but I do have a secret heart's desire. I've always wanted to do something illuminated, like Byzantine.'
>
> I did the whole thing, and there was a lot of work involved. Every time I got an assignment or went to school to work, and got stuff from the files, Edna Brandenburg would have a black person bring it, stay with me. . . Next time, another one, never the same one, for three months, at least, before the book came out. They were so talented, they were so nice to me. I doubt very much if she coached any of

them on how to accept me or how to get on with me or anything. They were just there, doing something from school, with somebody else who was doing something from school. And they became wonderful friends, and I thought, 'They are marvelous. They are better than half of the people I know.' It was so exciting. I didn't think of it as a revolution, but it did change my life and my thought.

People will say, 'Can you get on with the blacks?' I say, 'They are my *friends*. I never judge them, never by color. It doesn't exist anymore for me.' In fact, I once told someone that I think the Lord made the blacks, the red Indians and the whites, so that they would intermarry and become a beautiful gold-color skin. And I believed that.

I had a similar awakening of Miss Brandenburg's doing that also involved the school scrapbook. When I was in fifth grade, I made some tabletop photographs of paper designs and wooden letters that could be used as title pages for sections of the book. Miss Brandenburg immediately accepted them and then surprised me by saying, "Would you like to become our school photographer?" The job description included taking group photos in the classrooms, selling prints to the students as well as going on trips and making photos for the school scrapbook. I spent weeks in and out of my sixth grade classroom, and curiously, I remember more of what went on in class from sixth grade than from former or later years. Reading and math took hold in me that year.

Miss B. took a risk in allowing me to roam freely in school. She did not hire a professional photographer as often the next year. I rose to the invitation and, for a sixth grader, gave an acceptable performance. This was indeed fortunate, because the school superintendent, I later learned from Miss Brandenburg, did not support women as principals and wanted to replace them with men.

Simon Blackwell

Brother Put has strong images of Blackwell:

I could talk all night about Simon Blackwell. Blackwell was a delightful man, a black man, articulate, and very intelligent. I'm not sure how much education he had, whether he even got through high school, but he was a cool dude as I saw him at that time. I think he traveled in a fairly fast crowd. He played the horses. He had girlfriends. I believe that he played bridge. He certainly played cards. We used to spend a lot of time talking in the kitchen. He would tell me some of his stories. We'd talk, and I found him a good friend. And he'd cheer me up if things were tough or if something was going on and my love life wasn't going very well. Not that I had much love life.

Put paused, then went on:

I know that he used to battle Mom. They used to have fights. And he was pretty good. He stood up to her. After he left he'd come to visit, years later.

I saw him when I was living in New York. He was driving a cab. I know he drove a cab in the Newark-Chatham area. I heard he died. I was out of medical school at that time. It was like losing a friend, because I always liked Simon. He was never Simon, he was always Blackwell.

Neighbor Faith Stranad also remembered Blackwell:
Blackwell was something else again. He really was. He would come over and visit and tell us what was going on with him. I was so impressed at having a neighbor who was a chauffeur when he put on his chauffeur's hat, and a butler when he served the dinner and cooked it. And he had a wonderful manner. Nice looking, he could go anywhere.

During my junior high school years, I tried to get out of the house early on Thursdays, the help's day off. Any delay would mean having to listen to Mom begin her predictable lament over the failures of the help. I could count on Mom getting down on her knees to root around in the kitchen cupboards looking for greasy pans. Often she found one, and the rant would begin, continuing upon the help's return.

Once I joined in the thrashing of the help. Seeing grime on a mirror, I wrote in the haze with my finger, "clean." Blackwell recognized my uneven script. He caught me when Mom wasn't around: "Hey, Bob, did you write on that mirror? Don't you know to talk to me? [long pause] Don't you ever, *ever*, <u>ever</u> do a thing like that again, to nobody. You hear? Do you hear me? Do you hear ME?"

Blackwell scared me. I had been moving along doing my parents' bidding, learning their moves. Blackwell, who had watched me grow up, saw his moment and took it. As an employee of my mother, he must have considered the consequences before letting me have it. I never doubted he meant what he said; he was in a painful but controlled rage. Perhaps for the first time, I saw Blackwell as a person deserving of extraordinary respect, regardless of race and station. In that instant he took me beyond any inkling I had of respect for anyone else or myself. Though he frightened me, I must have sensed he had *my* best interest at heart, so I didn't tell Mom, who would have summarily fired him.

Blackwell gave me a different image of what I could be. I had to learn to talk to people as I would want to be spoken to. I had to begin to regard every person as worth a lot more than I had been accustomed to thinking. My father's teaching about the racial and social inferiority of people of color was forever undone after Blackwell confronted me.

Nellie Gordon Blasius, A.G.O.

Mrs. Blasius was the Dean of the New Jersey Chapter of the American Guild of Organists and served as organist and choir director for Central Presbyterian Church all the years I lived in Summit. At Christmas and Easter she added trumpets and trombones to the organ's voices to support the professional soloists who complemented the volunteer choir.

When Mrs. Blasius heard me play the timpani for a high school concert, she invited me to join in the church's music for Easter. I jumped at the opportunity and got permission to carry the high school's drums across the street to the church. At the monthly meeting of the church Session, Mrs. Blasius announced my inclusion in the Easter ensemble. Elder Robert LeMare surprised the gathering by rising to his feet, shaking his finger at Mrs. Blasius and saying, "You will *not* turn my church into a cabaret."

Taken aback, Mrs. Blasius paused a moment then responded, "Well then, I guess you'll have to find yourselves a new organist." The matter was left there, unresolved, and Mrs. Blasius helped me jockey the timpani into position high above the pulpit next to the organ console. On Easter Mrs. Blasius pulled out the stops, I pounded the timpani, the trombones and trumpets punched the congregation in the chest, and the voices soared over us all. Mrs. Blasius overwhelmed the opposition.

But she might not have been given the opportunity to do so. The elders might have let her go or tried harder to force her to let me go.

Mrs. Blasius told me of Mr. LeMare's objections at a rehearsal the week before as I stood at the timpani next to the organ. She knew the elders all knew me; I had recently appeared before them as a candidate for the ministry, and Elder LeMare had taken an interest in me. Had he called me, I might have taken the prudent road and declined to play. But when Nellie told me, I realized very clearly how much I wanted to play in *her* band. And I did. Can a church organist become a model of courage? Yes, indeed.

Master Sergeant Frangene Cooper

One of my memories of the nineteen-forties is of men and women getting on and off trains in uniform. The military were an ever-present part of community life. Armistice Day and Decoration Day were duly noted with civic gatherings. But what most attracted me was not the speeches and ceremonies or the ritual firing of rifles and cannons, but the bands. It was the syncopated street beats.

I had learned good stick form and the basic rudiments with Mr. Fulmer in elementary school. He taught me to read drum music before I could enjoy a book. In those years street beats reached their highest expression in school marching bands—before clean syncopations were trampled by rock drumming. But unless the lead drummer—the bass drummer—maintained the beat precisely, the syncopations of all the other drums lost their power. The best beatkeeper of all those years was my classmate Gene Cooper. When, after a separation of almost 40 years, I introduced him to my wife, Toni, Gene said:

> We were together all four years. Bob was the tallest member of the drum section, and then James, and then Jody, my brother, and then Morris, James Grant, me and then Mike Yannotta. Everybody worked hard. We got out there in the afternoons and went through practice and drill.

Gene, by his own account, was not a saint:

> There's not a member of my family, save maybe my brothers, who didn't have me on a fast track to Sing-Sing. And then I got in the band, the drum section, then playing on TV, playing in clubs, playing in homes. Then attitudes started changing. My parents made a challenge to me. They said if you make the honor roll, we'll buy you a set of drums. Well, I made the honor roll. I got my drums, and I got off the honor roll.

Not only did we drummers bow to Gene, the entire band was excited by him. Drumming on the leading edge of Gene's authoritative beat was not a challenge for me, but Gene wanted more.

At the close of one Thursday afternoon practice session across a dusty baseball diamond, Gene announced, "And if you're not going to clean your white bucks, don't bother to show up Saturday. I've had it with you guys not looking sharp." Gene recalled:

> We had a good drum section; we had a sharp drum
> section. I think of all the schools in the Conference,
> we had the sharpest-dressed band, and I hated like
> heck to see us looking sharp and our shoes not
> clean. So, in order to bring out what we had as a
> drum section, shoes needed to be shined. All of it is
> part of the music, and one had to complement the
> other. That's why I figured, hey, let's really look
> sharp and let's keep the shoes up, too. People see
> you, and you're not going to sound good if you
> don't look good. And we sounded good.
>
> And at almost every football game, at every
> parade, when people heard those drums, people
> started running. They wanted to see the band;
> they wanted to hear the drums. We were it, you
> know? How many bands did you see that let the
> drums do what they wanted to do? You didn't
> have that many. We led the band on the field.
> When it came time to play the Star Spangled
> Banner, the drums were out there by themselves.
> And we pulled the band.

One of the drummers, Mike Yannotta, resisted Gene's attempts to bring us into line. Gene reminisced:

> Mr. Hannaford left me in charge of the band. And we were playing a song, and I was up there with the little stick, flagging away, and Mike started clowning around. And it made me upset. And I came down off of the bandstand, and Mike didn't back down. And I pushed him, which I shouldn't have done. I should have maintained my cool. I think to this day I'm the only student leader who never led the band during the Spring Concert. But hey, I goofed. And I accepted it. And you know, nowadays, had it happened, people would start howling 'racism' and all that. But no, it wasn't that. He punished me, and rightfully so. I deserved what I got because I should have been able to maintain my cool. I shouldn't have pushed Mike Yannotta.

Ironically, considering his racist attitudes, it was my dad who prepared me to meet Gene's demands. When I was seven, Dad sawed, drilled, carved, sanded, and stained a rifle stock, fit a broom stick barrel on top with small screw eyes for sights, then taught me the manual of arms. Dad's teaching about good order and discipline was part of learning how "to polish up the handle on the big front door," as the operetta lyrics go. It could lead to economic and social advancement. Well, Dad never knew I shined my shoes at Gene's command. Gene continued:

Bob impressed me as a rich kid from the uppercrust side of town. Sometimes we would have fights, and it was the rich kids against the poor kids. It wasn't the white kids against the black kids. Because the rich kids were all white. The poor kids were black and white. So, 'we're going to have a fight today: it's the rich kids against the poor kids. Over on this side, ladies and gentlemen, you've got five white and five black poor kids. On this side here you've got ten rich kids.'

And there was no such thing as color. Poor kids against the rich kids, and it was usually over because everybody was glad that nobody threw the first punch. But Bob impressed me: he was tall; he reflected the image. By that I mean being from wealth. Because of the way he carried himself: tall, stately and everything. But when you put him in the drum section and you strapped a drum on him, he was just like everybody else. We were all just like each other. There was no difference.

And whatever anybody tried to see, they saw it in each one of us. And that's why to this day I feel that's what made us all such a good drum section: we all reflected each other, but we reflected each other in a positive way. I think people saw this. Because when people heard the drums, they started running. You know, they wanted to see. And here we come, and here we are, and there we go.

After high school graduation, while I accompanied my parents to summer parties, where they bragged about my Ivy League and ministerial future, Gene enlisted in the Air Force to train as Air Police. He then went to Morocco and on to Vietnam to rid the world of Vietcong. For forty years our lives diverged, until I went searching and found him.

I know these five people of my past—Sara Sykora, Edna Brandenburg, Simon Blackwell, Nellie Blasius, Gene Cooper—as risk-takers in events that involved me. These folks were flat-out provocative of my truer self. They shine so brightly in my consciousness because they plainly acted out of something inside themselves. In the days we were together, I did not know what "this little light of mine" meant, and it took a while for me to stop backing into a future I was expected to fulfill. I did not know what it meant to turn around and walk forward into a future that I could do better.

Although she had been elected to Phi Beta Kappa, Sara Sykora was required to wear a uniform, signaling servant status, when she found a job as my "governess." It wasn't until years later that I began to realize what a godsend she had been in my formative years. As I discovered the world around me, she aided and abetted my curiosity. To Mom's dismay, she accompanied Dad to Phi Beta Kappa chapter meetings in New York.

7.

Perhaps these little notes will set you right. I hope so as you have seemed most unfair in your judgment. I cannot stand unfairness. CoCo
P.S. over

Principal Brandenburg dealt an unanticipated blow to us boys who found Margie Romach's pigtails irresistible. Thereafter, the very thought of pigtails caused us to recoil. Miss Brandenburg was equally wise in approaching every student with the excitement of learning and gaining competence. She got to know our parents and acted as our advocate.

Parents, waiting to talk with the principal, were entertained by the scrapbook and the African tapestry.

When, in fifth grade, I brought Miss Brandenburg these chapter title photos for the scrapbook that sat outside her office, I had no idea she would reward me by asking if I'd like to become the school photographer. The concept didn't exist in my mind, but it took shape rapidly as I found myself selling classroom photos to the kids.

Blackwell was never at a loss to entertain others, to entertain himself, or to comment on any foolish idea I might have voiced. He brought a sense of performance to everything he did. It was never who he was, rather, it was always the part he was playing, whether he was cooking, serving, cleaning, chauffeuring, teaching me pinochle, or listening to our problems. This was how he upheld his identity against Mom's frequent criticism.

After my grandmother's death, Mom "let him go" in favor of the English couple who had cared for Nanny. Blackwell then drove a cab, visiting occasionally to check up on us, or go for a sail with my brother.

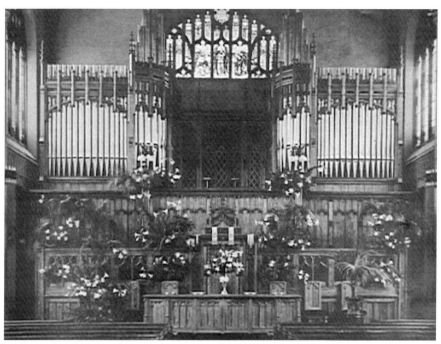

Presbyterian architecture focused attention on the Bible and its interpretation, hence the elevated central pulpit. Above the pulpit at Central Presbyterian Church was the choir loft, from which hymns were led and anthems sung out to the congregation. Organist Nellie Blasius' addition of timpani to the Easter services caused quite a ruckus.

Photos on this page used by permission of the Summit Historical Society

Mrs. Blasius taught me there are political dimensions to music-making, and one should always be ready to take a stand when challenged.

The esprit of Summit High School had its pinnacle in the Marching Band, where students who didn't see each other on most days came together. College, business, and general curriculum students played well. Parades were staged after every football victory. Throughout the year the band played at the beginning and end of Friday school assemblies, as well as in seasonal concerts and for town events.

Drum Major Gene Cooper headed the band as well as the drum section, a cheerleader for the former, a taskmaster for the latter. When the cadence wasn't just right, you heard about it. When the marching wasn't just right, you heard about it. When it was time to get to work again, you knew.

After graduation from Summit High School Gene Cooper enlisted in the Air Police. His first assignment was outside Casablanca. When he learned his three brothers were headed for Vietnam, he volunteered to go, too, serving there between nineteen sixty-six and nineteen seventy-one. Based in Taiwan, he married and returned to the U.S. after President Carter announced the One China policy.

When we were reunited in the early nine-teen-nineties, Gene had retired as Security Supervisor for the Bell Labs at Murray Hill and gone on to work at the Veterans Administration Hospital at Lyons, New Jersey. Our histories couldn't have been more diverse, yet Gene had no difficulty understanding what we were each up against in our Summit years. In very different ways, the SHS Marching Band was important basic training for both of us.

Hand Drumming
—DRUMMING TO EMBRACE THE TERROR

Shifting Awareness

If I likened my vocation to drumming, I would say I've moved away from the rudiments of marching bands. I've hung up my field drum and picked up a hand drum. Hand drummers do not usually wear uniforms that advertise their tribe. Their drums come in a variety of sizes and shapes, some to be carried, others stationary, and they drum with the several parts of their hands: fingers flat, heels of their palms, full hand slaps, and finger tips. Where field drumming summons allegiance, hand drumming calls for action. The former is about marching (as to war), the latter is about dancing (and singing your songs). If my family's rudiments were designed to attune me to a life in their society apart from others, the patterns of hand drumming are used to pick up everyone, including the most alienated, wherever she or he might be.

A few years ago I had a reunion with a couple I had thought I'd lost as friends because of family decisions I'd made back in the nineteen-seventies in Fitchburg, Massachusetts, when I was their pastor. Many years later I received a Christmas card from them. Shirley and Bill Moulton now live amid the Alleghenies where I visited them. In Fitchburg we had lived across the street from one another. Shirley explained:

> During that time, the people in the Blossom Street area, our neighbors, didn't find Bob and his family much different from the rest of us who were there. It was a neighborhood where people prided themselves in having a profession. We lived in an apartment across the street from Bob, and we had an Italian landlady. She was the first Catholic Italian to move into the WASP neighborhood, and she felt very much like she had been discriminated against when she moved into that neighborhood. She spent a great deal of time observing what was going on in the neighborhood, and the Brodsky house became a marvelous attraction for her.
>
> As time went on, they had a young girl over there who had some problems, and they brought her into their home. Mrs. Costa, our landlady, was just flabbergasted: 'Why are they bringing those kinds of people up the hill?' I reminded her that that was Bob's profession. He was a minister. Ministers do things like that. And, of course, after that young girl left, then there were more hippie-type people coming to the Brodsky household, which was very disconcerting for her.
>
> There was a particular young girl by the name

of Rosalie that in Mrs. Costa's mind was the Jezebel of Fitchburg. She started questioning what kind of a minister was Bob Brodsky, and why is his wife allowing him to have those types of people in their household? Then black people started coming up over the hill. Mrs. Costa was just beside herself, and she would spend long hours sitting in a lawn chair by her window so she could see what was going on at the Brodsky's house.

Anyone that showed up there after 9:00 at night, for sure, they were black. It became an obsession with her. Her threat to the neighborhood was, 'Well, I'm going to sell my place, and I'm going to sell it to somebody black. And anyone that's offended me for the last fifty years, this will be the pay back.' I remember one morning her calling me, and she was just beside herself. The evening before a young gentleman with a big white cowboy hat and cowboy boots had showed up and knocked at the Brodskys' door. Bob had allowed him in, and in her mind, he was black. There was no question about it. She was just petrified. She was having an anxiety attack and insisted that I call over to the Brodskys that morning and find out who that person was. So I called over and explained to Bob Mrs. Costa's concerns, and he said, 'Well, no, there wasn't anybody black here last night. I did have a young white man come to my door, who was having a bad time with some drugs he was on, and I took him to Burbank Hospital.' I got off the phone and explained to Mrs. Costa that the person was not black; I certainly did not explain to her that the person was on drugs. She really would have had heart failure. I could not convince her that that individual was not black.

We got more involved with the Brodskys and in the activities that Bob was participating in in the community and on our street. He was a champion for the young people in our neighborhood. He allowed them to sit on his stone wall; he allowed them to do their own thing. He encouraged them to participate with the elderly people in our neighborhood. He took them on little escapades with him. If he was involved in something going on at the church, he would run out to the wall and grab several teenagers and encourage them to come and participate in what his current project was. Perhaps he was taking them down into the slums of Fitchburg. And these were white, middle-class children who didn't have this exposure. And I know for a fact that most of the children who sat on the wall and were exposed to Bob learned a lot of great lessons about participating in their community and interacting with people who were not like them.

Back then I felt my friendship with the Moultons was as solid as anyone could hope for. Bill, in particular, was ahead of me in creating ways to confront social barriers. He recalled:

> The culmination of the Sunday School activity came on Children's Day, a time for the Sunday school kids to show off what they had learned— what they were all about—to the congregation in the sanctuary. Our kids felt that the issues of blacks and whites in society was so big a part of what they had done in their Sunday School, they wanted to demonstrate this issue in front of the congregation.
>
> We knew there were great risks if we allowed them to do what they wanted to do. They had different views than their parents had, of course, and I must point out, the makeup of this class that Shirley and I had, was becoming more and more black. We started out with the offspring of the usual congregation parents, but the classroom became such an interesting place for kids to get together, that it became a hangout for kids whose parents were not going to that church. And we ended up with a lot of kids who were coming from the black community who had no place else to go where they could do relevant discussion.
>
> So, the makeup of our class changed. We had people who were, according to the congregation members, rather 'uninvited attendees.' Nonetheless, they were welcome in our group because they were

helping those kids, regular church members, deal with things that were important to them, too.

On Children's Day, we talked about what they wanted to do. They decided they wanted to let the parents know how they felt about blacks and whites. In the end, they appeared—we all appeared—upstairs in the sanctuary with faces that were painted with either green or blue, which was a statement about how unimportant either black or white was. We spread ourselves throughout the congregation, some in the middle, some in corners, and delivered a message. In responsive reading style—there was a leader who would start the message, and others would respond with the following line—the kids delivered to the adult members of the congregation the Declaration of Independence in a way that the congregation had never heard before, in a way that I think only one person recognized as the Declaration of Independence.

Many in the congregation were concerned that this was some new revolutionary message that the kids had made up. It struck fear in the hearts of some, who thought that the church was going much too far when, in fact, the kids were only giving back to them what we had fundamentally agreed upon—our covenant of over 200 years of the struggle of all men, all women—all people—in a way that was powerful for them and very dramatic.

During my years as pastor to the Moulton family in Fitchburg, I was not aware of how far away I stood from a typical Protestant ministry—of smoothing ruffled feathers and recruiting seekers into Christian creeds—toward a ministry of active intervention with the rigorous compassion of Jesus. But other people were.

The night before nationally-known birth control advocate Bill Baird began serving a jail term for publicly giving a condom to a minor during a lecture in Massachusetts, I invited him to speak to families with teenagers at our church about his views. He did, then went to prison. Some church members thought birth control was strictly a family matter, and the church should not be involved (as Catholics had been).

Drug use among teens was very much a concern among parents at the close of the nineteen-sixties, and during a junior high youth group meeting at the church, the local police conducted a drug bust, scaring the bijesus out of the kids. The cops "found" some grass. After being hauled off to the local jail in paddy wagons, the students were informed it was a put-up job (by the youth group staff and myself) and were given a brief lecture on the costs of using illegal drugs. All the parents were told about it beforehand, but when others in the congregation got wind of it, they again said the church should leave it to the parents.

There were many black families in Fitchburg and the sur-rounding towns, mostly related to the Army's Fort Devens. To church members they were practically invisible. All over the United States in the nineteen-sixties black people were letting their hair grow. White folks were scared; things got pushy. Scared or not, I decided we should have a festival to celebrate the gifts and talents of black people in America to give the whites something else to think about. Many people in the church participated in the planning and arrangements. Late in the evening before the festival the Fitchburg Fire Department volunteered to help hoist an 8'x16' orange Day-Glo silhouette of a Nubian princess to the church tower. During the festival, art and sculpture from Boston Black Artists were displayed in the church school auditorium. In the Aubuchon Hardware parking lot next door, a Roxbury boutique put on a fashion show. A bold black poet recited his baddest verse from a small outdoor stage where in the evening drummers and dancers from Boston put on a show. Black folks gathered from all around our area. While waiting in line for fried plantain (with coconut), an elderly church member told me this was the first time she had ever "felt outnumbered at her own church." The aroma of West Indian cooking permeated the church fellowship hall for weeks afterward. The church boards supported the festival as long as it hadn't cost the church anything. So, when my co-minister heard I had charged a rental truck to my personal credit card, he protested to the governing boards of the church. I didn't think it a big deal, but it became one.

In the fall of 1969 a call went out from the National Council of Churches for congregations across America to toll their bells for five minutes on the Saturday after Thanksgiving in memory of the Vietnam war dead. I had never spoken from the pulpit of my opposition to America's participation in Vietnam's civil war, but I had led prayers for peace during the intercessory part of Sunday worship. Our church had a tall stone tower with a very large bell. I climbed the ladders and tolled the bell. The following morning, as I entered the choir robing room, the mood was unusually somber. There wasn't a hint of the usual frivolity. As everyone awaited my customary prayer for the choir (similar to what football teams do before a game), choir member Rose Goodspeed spoke out: "Who rang the bell?" "I did," I said. "Well then, you ought to be hanged," she replied. No one else spoke to soften her attack. Clearly, my act was perceived as giving aid and comfort to an enemy. Suddenly, I was back in Dr. Buschman's office, except now I was sitting in his chair. I felt scared, angry, and sad. Two hundred yards from the church, a defense contractor was making devices that were maiming and killing men, women, and children from the air, and church members were pissed off over my ringing a bell in memory of all the dead? It was apparent I hadn't been able to lead church members to embrace the enemy; it was too big a risk. I left the church and the pastoral role the following spring and never felt regret for leaving.

Although I left the congregation, I did not leave the city, and I continued to be called upon to intercede in trouble spots. One night at supper I received a call from a man I could hardly understand. He said he was being refused admission to the local porno theatre because he was from Puerto Rico. Would I come and speak with the manager? When I arrived, I found a large family waiting under the marquee. The manager explained to me he didn't want these people in his theatre because the preceding week they had talked and laughed a lot during the show. The family said this was their first visit. I negotiated that I would go with them if the manager would let us into the show, and he did. The only disruption was from an aged Anglo woman who left her seat to swing her handbag toward others who laughed or talked.

The photographic skills I had acquired early, propelled by Miss Brandenburg's encouragement, enabled me to illustrate connections between people of diverse backgrounds and opinions. As Lafayette Grisby said to me much later, "As happens in life many times, irony steps in and has a joke on us." My efforts to enable cultural appreciation in Fitchburg through a Christian institution—an institution commissioned to such work—were blowing in the wind, but through photography I could at least continue to work at it. Of course, I would appear very different to those who knew me in ministerial mode. When I would meet members of my former congregation, the irony of my shift in jobs would rise up and dance about me. Though I was ill-suited to do what I needed to do as a person through an institution created to do this work, I could do it through a venue that had a variegated reputation. It did not escape notice that most photographers of merit were Jews. Imagine a photo of a bunch of Protestant ministers, then a bunch of photographers (including filmmakers), and you'll see what I mean.

The events of September 11, 2001 and, particularly, the subsequent actions of the federal government have changed the way many Americans view the world and themselves, unfortunately, not for the better. Terrorism is on everyone's mind. Since a marksman created havoc from the University of Texas bell tower in Austin in 1966, killing sixteen and wounding thirty-one local residents, I've been aware of how little effort it takes to panic civil society. A civil society is a fragile organism.

My own civility was once severely tested during a rash of tire slashing and car radio thefts on my street when I lived in a poor neighborhood near Harvard University. My bed in the window bay of the third floor apartment abutted the sidewalk, and I kept a brick on the bedside bookcase to hurl down on anyone I saw vandalizing a car. I judged the deeds were being perpetrated by a gang of Portuguese teenagers, but when I approached some of the kids who hung out in my neighborhood, I learned of another suspect: a solitary kid of my own ethnic group who lived within view of my back porch. The Portuguese kids were hoping to catch him in his acts so they could beat the crap out of him or turn him in to the cops and vindicate their own reputations. So, I took my brick away.

Taking all this in, when, in Oklahoma City, the Murrah Federal Building was blown up, killing one hundred sixty-eight people, including the occupants of a child care center, when the twin towers fell, when airliners have been blown out of the sky, I have been horrified—truly horrified—but not surprised, and I am less inclined to rush to judgment or take inappropriate actions.

At the end of that terrible week of September 11th, our small town planned an evening candlelight worship on the town common. When I learned of it, my immediate response was to seek out Muslim families in our community and invite them to attend the service with me. I first asked the folks in the drug store, but they couldn't think of any. Leaving the pharmacy, I saw Kevin Barry, our police chief, directing traffic around the funeral of a family who died on one of the airliners, and I asked him. Chief Barry had known me since I came to town. He had run a check on my wife, Toni, and me when we signed up for the Rowley Block Program. He seemed not surprised by my inquiry and suggested I ask the guys at our convenience store. I had assumed they were Hindus, but when I spoke with the clerk, he told me he was from Bangladesh and was Muslim. I told him I would stop by before the gathering and bring him with me. He told me he would have to check with his boss. At the appointed hour I arrived to find the boss making a sign for the front door: "Closed for 1 hour." Jul, the clerk, and Elias, the store owner, walked across Route 1A with me and joined the crowd. They seemed calm, but I was nervous, aware that feelings were running high against brown-skinned people. I led us to a place where we could stand behind a couple of cops. The worship proceeded in broadly Christian terms with one of our selectmen assisting the Catholic priest and Protestant clergyman. When the worship ended, Elias turned to me and said, "I have never been to Christian worship, and there are many things just like in Islam. You know, Jesus is considered holy in our faith. Yes, the Koran speaks of him a number of times." Several townsfolk spoke warmly to Jul and Elias as we walked back across the road.

Bringing Elias Talukder and Julfikar Kadar to the religious gathering was a very small thing, yet an important one. I am grateful to them for accepting my request. I feel I have to talk across differences much more than I'm doing. It's not enough to be friendly toward people who differ from my own kind. I believe we have to find ways to share important moments in one another's lives, however momentary, where sharing can be realized among all parties, where people feel it and will remember it. Since geographical isolation is no longer feasible, I must overcome the subtle disdain I practice on others: the shunning of people because of class, trade, gender, religion, race, sexual orientation, nonviolent criminality, endowment, or poverty. I saw my mother, like my father, overcome her alienating attitudes time and again to become seriously involved with the families of servants, lending money and helping them sort out family problems. They, in turn, helped her when chronic alienation got the best of her. A black child was named after my mom in gratitude.

I must never be afraid of risking myself to empower people as the Others did to me. This has nothing to do with agreeing with them but of standing up for others, as CoCo did for my mom's cook Hilma. I don't know what happened to CoCo upon delivering those scraps of paper with her indictment of Mom, but I know how she felt, how she carried herself as a person before and afterward. I know what her words could have meant to Hilma (if she ever heard them).

Any of those risk-takers in my early life could have lost his job if I complained about them to those who had authority over them. So, what was my responsibility? Did I do the responsible thing by bending to Blackwell's and Cooper's injunctions? *Should* I have played the timpani in church? Seemingly insignificant, questionable acts sometimes figure large in the future of things.

Doing the Unexpected to Others

The social alienation experienced worldwide today is a product of many forces—the domination of lobbyists over political life, the selling of everything, the deepening fundamentalist currents of protest, the constant awareness of the variety of weapons of mass destruction—to name a few. The older demons—corruption, war-making, feckless leadership—seem as much in evidence as ever. Against this backdrop an individual is likely to feel diminished. Worldwide recognition of personal accomplishment of any sort vanishes in seconds. Excellence is a flash in the pan. Ideology aside, it is not hard to see how terror-making has vocational appeal. My sense is that trying to directly defeat any of these demons, including terror-making, is futile. What is not futile is any effort to help another person to use his talent as a supportive member of a community.

My experiences as a pastor left me with the puzzling conviction that the majority of people who call themselves religious are ideologically ill-equipped to deal with actions of others they don't like or see as dangerous to society. They retreat into name-calling to distinguish themselves from offenders, which has the effect of isolating them. Their ability to weave offenders back into the torn tapestry of society is limited by the distinctions they have made. They want their tapestries to look like they did before they were offended, but they never will. As I see it, this is where personal beliefs and acts of faith part company—or need to.

Images of "faith" and "belief" have been confused for centuries. Faith, as I know it, can be seen only in actions. For me, Christian faith is grounded in the practice of forgiveness. God forgives us; we must forgive others. That is the fundamental that Jesus returns to again and again. The proof of forgiveness is known only through actions. Forgiveness trumps all statements about judgment and punishment (Matthew 18:21). The religious authorities lost patience with Jesus over his position (Mark 11:25-33). When church fathers added an ascription of God's power onto the end of the Lord's Prayer, it further weakened a request about forgiveness that comes to us in that prayer, "forgive us our sins as we forgive those who sin against us." Do you believe that God does not forgive all sin? Sin is an ever-recurring experience; only the power of the Almighty overcomes it, and God overcomes it with forgiveness. Jesus took to himself the unqualified power to forgive heinous sins (e.g.: adultery, John 8 and for background see Mark 10 and Luke 16). He did this as "the son of man." Christians call Jesus the "Son of God." Does this weaken the commandment that we also forgive all sin?

Whatever people say about the beliefs they hold, their true beliefs are revealed through their actions. The act of forgiving sins speaks of humility before God—if you will, the most direct connection to the Final Authority. Or, to put it another way, if you want to be connected with God, you don't fight your neighbor or seek to punish him for his sins. I call the five Others in my life "persons of faith" because the risks they took in my presence revealed them as persons who took actions to enrich the life of him they were dealing with—me. I have no idea of their individual beliefs, but I have a sense of who they are at their core—in their souls—because of how they stood before me. Risking yourself before others defines you as a person of depth, by which I mean a person of faith.

When I return to the Bible, I find Jesus considering the actions of people as well as their witness to his own authority. Jesus turned on its head the doctrine of salvation by obedience to religious laws. Righteousness lay in the free deeds of ordinary people, not in their obedience to religious laws. He pointed to certain acts of non-Jews, calling them acts of faith, likening them to the power of tiny mustard seeds to grow into eleven-foot-tall trees. This is the power I recall in the Others; they surprised me by the authority they exercised. When people challenged Jesus' authority to say or do things, he responded, "Though you don't believe me, believe the works, that you may know and believe that God is in me, and I in him" (John 10:38).

Most of the terrorists of history have been motivated by perceived acts of power used against their tribes. They attack the people who are kin to the powerful. Combating terrorism requires that we identify and address the source of their craziness. No small risk. The alternative is more terrorists if there is truth to their cause. As far as I know, Jesus did not have to deal with today's brand of terrorism, but in one of the most powerful Gospel stories, Jesus addresses a crazy man living in a cemetery near the Sea of Galilee (Mark 5: 1-20, Luke 8:26-39). The mad man is beset by "demons," and Jesus addresses the multiple claims on his personality. The story is fantastical (the demons enter a stampeding herd of pigs who rush headlong into the sea), but the point couldn't be clearer: the guy has been taken over by terrors (plural is their nature). Once cleared of the demons, he calms down.

Terrorists are consumed by their ideologies. Ideologues do not ask questions. They have to be called into question on their own ground. The Great Satan is a many-headed monster, absorbing their attention and talents. Unlike the founding fathers of our country, they are unable to declare themselves free and independent and do whatever it takes to be free and independent. They are unable to focus their energy for the good of others; they use others, they put others in harm's way, and they do not accept responsibility for the harm they cause. All ideologues tend to share these characteristics.

But if our desire is to knit up the raveled fabric of society, the offenders have to be led to participate. Forgiveness is without limits but nevertheless has expectations: turn from your harmful ways and find ways to do good to others. Forgiveness without expectations does not reflect the human condition. Forgiveness without hope is foolishness.

We are connected to one another by hopes and expectations. They appear unrealistic, but they are valid connections, two-way connections. The forgiven one, if he has given up on all but terror-making, must be led to put aside destructive acts and practice hopefulness.

Terrifying as it is, the kidnapping strategy as practiced by some Iraqis is a step away from the vortex of suicide bombing. Dialogue is impossible with a suicide bomber, but the kidnapper is inviting dialogue, and therein lies an opportunity to bring the alienated back into civil society. Kidnapping is a criminal act, to be sure; a horrific event in any community. People are snatched away, kidnappers' demands may be broadcast, but then the ball is in our court. The chance of the safe return of those kidnapped is dependent not only on the mood of the kidnappers but on how willing those in power are to risk themselves by entering into negotiations with the kidnappers. If any dialogue takes place with the kidnappers, there is an opportunity to begin reweaving the torn fabric of society. Is there any other way?

The mistake that powerful nations make with terrorists is not pursuing dialogue, not attempting to reconnect. The powerful either meet the kidnappers' demands or try to find them and kill them. These responses only serve to harden their ideologies, increase support for their methods, and allow them to feel justified in their acts. Better to forgive them their horrors, hear their complaints, deal with them, and in so doing name and call out their demons. Retaliation or "pacification" (as we've come to use the term) has no place in civil society. There are no shortcuts to the risk of dialogue if we are to avoid the consequences of destructive ideologies.

My opinion is not favored by a majority of my countrymen, who favor the "stern father" approach to human relations. In foreign policy this translates into militarism (or at least, the threat of militarism). With hardly an exception, we choose warlords to lead us, and we favor them as leaders of other nations. When given a chance to choose or support a different kind of political leadership, we have seldom done so. Warlords, even if they do not actually lead us into war, foster anger and resentment both at home and abroad. Those who feel put down by them find ways to get even. Yet, when men of a more cooperative disposition have risen above the crowd—as we've witnessed since the nineteen-sixties—they've been ridiculed, abused, and scorned out of proportion to their ordinary human follies, or simply cut down. Modern South Africa is a notable exception.

Not enough people want peace to outvote those who support the warlords; not yet, at least. Too many would rather suffer under and die for their warlord than allow the better selves of all of us to thrive. This is the message of that puzzling book at the end of the New Testament, the book called "The Revelation to John," which predicts an apocalypse. Others have figured out that it would be a long time until people would receive a prince of peace, that, in fact, we had to exhaust ourselves before we would be ready for faith.

You already know that by "faith" I do not mean acceptance of Jesus (or anyone else one might consider) as the messiah. I mean rock solid faith that we are put on this earth to risk ourselves to be connected to one another. In doing so we come to know life and power beyond anything that this world can grant us.

The warlords would have us believe that evil can be eradicated. I don't think so, but evil can be blanketed with good. We can never obliterate terrorism, but we can hold before it a taste of the love of God.

If you must cry, cry for those who still follow the warlords.

Who Are My Tribe?

While I was working as a pastor in New England, Mom and Dad gradually tired of trying to lead me in their path. I had become too liberal ("sympathetic" was Dad's word), involving myself too frequently with people they did not approve of. It became clear to me that while I was still very much a member of their family, welcome at holidays, I was something of an outcast for my associations and viewpoints. So, I began asking what tribe I belonged to, if any.

We are born into tribes, and their hold on us is profound. Poet Robert Frost wrote, "Home is the place where, when you have to go there, they have to take you in." And they usually do. For how long depends on how closely you're related, whether or not you share their values, and how well you can cook. Outward from blood relationships, tribalism, until quite recently, has extended through nationality, ethnicity, class, religion, and race. I find welcome in groups merely by mentioning my ancestry in Bohemia or Vienna, in Scotland, or in County Down. Without mentioning my name, I'm accepted by Russians because I look like them.

When I attend a family reunion, I'm asked to stir the specialness of my family more than the accident of it, and I try to make the best of what to me is often an awkward moment. There are people I hit it off with and people I don't, but it's rude not to interact with all the assembled members. I tend to seek out the quiet ones. I find safety in service. If I can perform a function—running errands, fetching food and drinks, setting up chairs, being a messenger, running a-v equipment, leading a song or offering one—I feel better. I was trained from infancy for such jobs. I'm uncomfortable at family reunions, perhaps because the importance of heritage was so drummed into me as a child. I know how much family reunions mean to some folks, but I was once stuck in the past, and I don't want to become stuck there again.

I now view my family and my tribe as distinct from each other. My family (after the dead ones, who remain clearly in memory) are my wife and my kids and their kids and my other near-relatives, with whom I try to stay in touch and be available. But my tribe is different. Beginning with the Others I've written about, they are the folks I call "the tribe that doesn't know itself." They are people who have understood me better than I understand myself. They are not necessarily "a better class of people," but when I am with them, they bring clarity to my life. They breathe fresh air into my psyche. Those five Others of my early years did this, and, in so doing, gave me a template that other people may fit into. They prepared me to identify folks who take risks so that others may have a sense of themselves. They and folks both after and before them are my community of faith.

Is it a surprise that the Others have become my tribe? The Others, who were so corrective of the values I grew up with, have become the most relevant group for me. My tribe are the ones who speak out when someone is questioning or challenging a well-intentioned flow of energy. I never know when one of my tribe will reveal himself by doing or saying something to that end. And of course, we recognize one another only by shared events.

Have I said why marching bands make me cry? I suspect you now know. I love marching bands, and I don't always cry when one parades past me.

For many years Shirley Moulton carried an image of me hiding from our long friendship. She was right, and told me of her dismay when we renewed the friendship after twenty-five years.

A steady force for fruitful integration of people in communities, Bill Moulton intervened in imaginative and positive ways when we were neighbors in Fitchburg, Massachusetts.

Afro-American Cultural Festival Held in Fitchburg

FITCHBURG — A festival to commemorate the cultural contribution of the contemporary black man was held here yesterday.

Citizens of Fitchburg in cooperation with Faith United parish sponsored Afro-American today. The festival was held from 11 a.m. to 10 p.m.

on the grounds behind the Main Street parish as well as in the church.

The Boston Negro Artists Association presented a 40-piece exhibit that included the work of 20 artists. Oil painting and prints were also on sale.

The Nubian of Boston offered African artifacts for

sale and sponsored a fashion show.

An African supper consisting of a chicken, onion, pepper and banana mixture was served and gave Fitchburg residents a taste of an exotic African dish.

Black Music, Inc. provided 'soul music' for dancing.

The Tom Gillison Dancers led the large crowd in dancing. The five members of the group are all members of the Montachusett chapter of the NAACP. They are Rosetta Lyle, Cynthia Lyle, Francine Gunther, Brenda Fountain and Sharon Collings.

Highlight of the day's activ-

ities were five appearances of Bill Jamsa and five of his students doing African drum simulations. Jamsa teaches drums at Fitchburg Music Store and finds the African rhythms fascinating.

"They are much more complex than other drum music," he said.

"In fact, they are usually far too complex for the Tin Pan Alley ear of the most of the public, so they tend to call them primitive and savage."

To this day very little prominence is given to minorities in New England apart from schools and large metro areas. Race, class, and historic tribalism remain barriers to opportunity, security, and friendships for many people.

When I returned to photography, some despaired that I'd left "my profession," but I knew that the world was more alive to me through photography than by any other medium. Pictures always bring people together— after a while. Pictures cause us to think differently about ourselves and others, sometimes for good, sometimes for ill. The pictures I make and the pictures I choose to work with expand awareness and opportunity. Life can't stand still amidst an ever-expanding photographic record.

Graffito on a bar window in Portland, Maine. There are reasons wars happen, not obvious to everyone. There are reasons people can be forced or drawn into fighting. When the pivotal reasons are addressed with understanding, the destruction of communities by war cannot happen. What are they, and who shall address them?

Elias Talukder (top) and Julfikar Kadar have taught me a lot about Bangladesh and Muslim ways. The culture they have brought to this part of the world is being honored through the friendships they have made. They are as much a part of our old New England town as anyone else.

My mother greatly respected Louise yet abused Hilma (on the left). CoCo intervened, risking her job to end the aggression by confronting Mom in her unfairness, and listing the important contributions Hilma was making to our family. I am acquainted with wars begun in the kitchen.

ACKNOWLEDGMENTS

When I showed some of my first writing about the Others to friends, they insisted I write more of myself into the work. This scared me, but I managed to slip some of my feelings into the text. Then I asked other friends for their comments. They, too, said I needed to write more of myself into the work, and they told me where.

Many times over years of writing I lost my way and had to backtrack to find the stories that led me off the trail and set them aside. I apologize to friends and family who granted me interviews but whose efforts did not find a place in this work: Donald Isaksen, the Reverend Don Purkey, and Peggy Morse Brodsky. Your stories, though not included, helped me to focus on things that needed to be written out. Your sentiments, if not your words, are embedded in the text.

I thank my wife and partner, Toni Treadway, without whose creative partnering, support, and forbearance this account wouldn't be anything like it is. I thank film archivist Andrea McCarty, who created text out of the video interviews, then read and commented on an early version of the text. I thank school chums and author-editor Marilyn Hughes Johnson, whose experienced eye greatly improved the text, and anthropologist-archeologist Lee Ellis Horne, whose comments and questions helped me to grow while writing. Artists Poli Marichal and Christine Downing, and producer Lisa Feinstein, brought the ears of different cultures to their readings. I thank them and Tamara Fish for her sharp-eyed review of the final text and many helpful suggestions. Archival photo restoration was accomplished by Linda McCausland in North Eastham, MA, and the design, reproduction, and production of the book are the work of Joan Ross and Jim Higgins of Lowell, MA, each one, a paragon of patience and skill.

Bob Brodsky
January 2005